The Cades Cove Story

Editing and Design by Paula A. Degen

The
Cades Cove
Story

A. Randolph Shields

GREAT SMOKY MOUNTAINS NATURAL
HISTORY ASSOCIATION
Gatlinburg, Tennessee

Library of Congress Catalog Card Number: 77-76729

NOTE ON AUTHOR: A. Randolph Shields was born in Cades
Cove on April 8, 1913, and lived there until age thirteen. He gradu-
ated from Maryville College and received a M.S. and Ph. D. from
the University of Tennessee. He worked as an elementary school
teacher, an aquatic and fisheries biologist, an associate professor of
Biology at Emory and Henry College and Roanoke College, an
instructor in botany at the University of Tennessee, and as a professor and chairman of the Department of Biology at Maryville
College in Maryville, Tennessee. He also served as director of the
Maryville College Environmental Education Center. He served six
summers as a ranger-naturalist in Great Smoky Mountains National
Park. Shields was intimate with the Great Smokies as a national
park and as the place where he was born and raised.

To all of the descendants of the pioneering Cades Cove families, with the hope that those of each succeeding generation will revere the memories of their heritage.

Contents

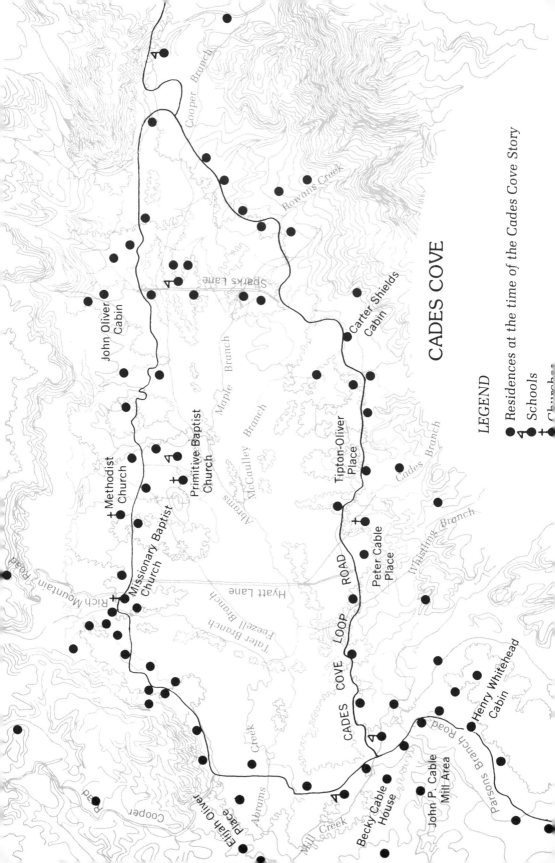

CADES COVE

LEGEND

Residences at the time of the Cades Cove Story

Schools

Churches

Preface

No story of Cades Cove can ever be complete, and I am presumptuous in calling this *the* Cades Cove story. Records are widely scattered and incomplete. However, I think it is time to begin to bring a semblance of a story out of what I have been able to find. Only the highlights can be expressed in a book of this size. The details of my research are on file in the park library at the Sugarlands Visitor Center near Gatlinburg.

This story could not have been written without the help of numerous people — people associated with several organizations, as well as just interested and cooperative individuals. I am especially indebted to the Natural History Association of the Great Smoky Mountains National Park for making it possible for me to take time out from my teaching to concentrate on the research essential to the story, and for seeing it through to publication. Many individuals of this organization went out of their way to help. Also, I thank the personnel of the Land Office of the National Park Service in Washington, D.C., and those of the National Archives who rendered valuable assistance. Office holders and employees at the Blount County Court House are appreciated for their courteous help. Many descendants of Cades Cove residents are to be considered partners in this venture. From them have come the photos, memories, and family histories that make this possible. I must express special thanks to Inez McCaulley Adams for her contribution of remembrances about her ancestral homestead.

For background history and much basic information, I am indebted to the writings of and to conversations with Miss Inez Burns. The papers of the late Professor Henry R. Duncan, long a Cades Cove history buff, which are deposited in the Lawson-McGhee Library in Knoxville, were also very helpful. Finally, I wish to thank Paula Degen for editing my material for publication.

Even with great care, errors will be made in transferring data, in drawing inferences from incomplete data, and in many other ways. For all of these, I alone accept the responsibility and plead for corrections from readers who discover them.

When I visit Cades Cove, I walk and meditate with the ghosts of the hundreds of people who shared the hardships and joys of that beautiful valley for more than a century, and without whom there would be no Cades Cove story. Thanks to all of them.

A Natural Phenomenon

I WONDER what the first white man who viewed Cades Cove from the mountain crest was thinking as his eyes scanned the broad, fertile valley that stretched before him. He must have felt that this secluded basin, surrounded by mountains and watered by clear creeks, would be discovered by others after him — that men would bring their families here to make their homes and live their lives on this land. Perhaps he sensed that these would be a special people, a people who would be bound together by the very mountains that separated them from the outlands, a people who would share a distinct community of experience.

Of course, we can never know what that first man was thinking. We will never know who he was nor what brought him to the cove. Much of the early history of Cades Cove remains a mystery. We do not even know how the cove got its name. The family name Cade is found scattered about east Tennessee, and even to Texas. However, as far as I know, there has been no attempt to trace the origin nor its probable relationship to Cades Cove. The name Cades Cove was known and used as a point of reference as early as the eighteenth century. Hugh Dunlap was issued a land grant by the State of North Carolina in 1794 for "5,000 acres in a place called Cades Cove." The name must go back beyond that date. There are several myths regarding its origin, but these have not been substantiated. Perhaps some day, someone will find an answer in the earliest survey records or in the archives of North Carolina or elsewhere, but for now the origin of the name remains a mystery.

There are things we do know about the beginnings of Cades Cove even without written history — things we can tell from the formation of the land, from the vegetation, and from unusual fossil deposits in the stone. A mountain cove, similar to its aquatic counterpart, is a low area, surrounded by mountains and having a single drainage outlet. At one time the area that includes Cades Cove was covered with a shallow sea. To the southeast was a low coastal range of very old rocks.

About 400 million years ago various units of the crust of the earth began moving towards each other, and the North American mass collided with that of Africa. This "collision" lasted for several million years, and its forces were tremendous. The eastern North American region was folded up and pushed northwestward for many miles, forming the mountain ranges we know as the Blue Ridge and the Great Smokies. The older rocks were pushed up and over the younger limestones, which had been deposited in the shallow sea, and began to break up. Streams cut and smoothed the surfaces. Near the front, the upper layer was shallow and in some places the streams finally eroded into the underlying limestone. As a result, the cove that would one day be called Cades came into being, as did Tuckaleechee and Wear's coves nearby.

While these mountains and coves were being shaped by the elements, the vegetation that now covers them was also developing from primitive ancestors. There is good evidence that during the great ice ages, the high mountains of the Smokies were treeless and ice-covered for the great part of each year, thawing and re-freezing, causing boulders to break away and tumble down the slopes. In this way the peaks were lowered rather rapidly during each ice age. As the ice receded, the glacier-front forest followed it northward and upward in the mountains. Remnants of this forest from the latest ice age still remain in the high Smokies. Evidence indicates that the vegetation that covers the slopes around Cades Cove has been in place throughout its developmental history. The magnolias and their relatives are the oldest flowering trees, but the conifers are the oldest woody plants in origin. The non-woody plants came along after the woody ones, the buttercup family being the oldest of these. Orchids, lilies, and grasses are the relative newcomers.

The mystique of such areas as Cades Cove lies to a great extent in the appreciation of their antiquity and of the forces of nature that formed them and clothed the mountain slopes and valley floors. Those phenomena created a barrier to man's arrival and settlement of Cades Cove, but once penetrated, they allowed a distinct mountain community to develop and thrive. Those same forces can eliminate all evidence of man's presence, if given enough time. We have to look very closely now to see where farms once were in many areas of the Great Smoky Mountains National Park, including Cades Cove, even after only forty years.

Taming the Land:
settlement of cades cove

*The story of Cades Cove is the story of the
community that existed in this rich valley for
115 years, between 1821, when families began
moving into the cove to settle, and 1936, when
the area became part of the Great Smoky
Mountains National Park. Who were the people
who came to make their homes here? What was
life like for them, somewhat separated from the
mainstream of American development, in this
secluded – though not isolated – mountain
area? What is our debt to those who sacrificed
their ancestral homes in order that we and the
generations to follow can know and share these
meadows and mountains?*

Cades Cove stood out from among the Great Smokies as land that could be tamed. Nature had created in the cove a flat mountain valley of fertile land that was attractive to an agrarian people. It was only a matter of time before pioneers on their way westward would stop here and stay. They would settle, clear the land, and raise their crops and livestock. As more people came, they would form governments, churches, schools, and community ties.

Blount County was established as a political entity in September, 1795, when it was voted into existence by the General Assembly of the Territory South of the Ohio River. A year later, Tennessee became a state. However, Cades Cove was not yet open for settlement. It was included in a sizable area that was still part of the Cherokee Nation. A few white settlers may have already been in the area, but no one could legally own land there until 1819 when the Cherokees relinquished their claim through the Calhoun Treaty.

As early as 1794 from North Carolina and in the early 1800s from Tennessee, several grants and entry rights had been issued for Cades Cove land, even though they could not be legally claimed. In March of 1821, William Tipton was granted two sections (1,280 acres) to consolidate several previous entries. Although William Tipton never lived in the cove, this was

Farming was the main support for the Cades Cove community. These Tipton-Oliver farm buildings were built by Col. J. W. H. Tipton in the 1870s and later bought by William H. Oliver.

the first recorded legal land title for Cades Cove following the Calhoun Treaty.

State grants continued to be issued through 1890, although those after about 1870 were for title confirmation only and not for new lands. In all, thirty-six land grants are recorded for Cades Cove from 1821 through 1890. The State of Tennessee usually required a fee of $1.00 per acre for land grants. A few grantees were also obligated to develop the mineral resources on their lands.

William Tipton, along with his brothers Abraham and Thomas, obtained possession of most of the valley floor, the best agricultural lands. The largest grants were to Charles and William Murray for 5,000 acres each in 1838. Much of this land was east of the cove, including the headwaters of the West Prong of Little River, but it did extend into the eastern part of the valley. The early grantees were, for the most part, speculators, but within a few years titles to the land rested in buyers who were more interested in settling in the cove. (See Appendix A for a list of recorded land grants for Cades Cove.)

Until 1836, the organized units of Blount County were militia companies, and all able-bodied men aged 21 through 50 belonged to these units. Cades Cove was known as Captain Absolum Wiseman's Militia, and Jacob Tipton was listed as a justice, a member of the county court.

The area was established as the Sixteenth Civil District of Blount County in 1836 and described as follows:

. . . including all the inhabitants in Cades Cove, and in the Chestnut Flats also all those living on or near the road from the Rich Gap to Cades Cove which bounds shall constitute the 16th District and we designate the house of Captain Jacob Tipton as the place for holding elections in the said district. (From the Minutes of the Blount County Court.)

The voters of each district elected a constable and two justices of the peace, or squires. The latter from all the county districts made up the county court. The local constable and squires kept the peace and handled most of the legal business of the district. This was especially so in Cades Cove, due to its relative isolation. In the cove, the justices of peace advised in neighborly squabbles, wrote wills, helped in making deeds, performed weddings, and aided in all normal legal matters. They were usually elected because they were the better educated and more experienced men. The constable was, for the most part, a man thought best able to keep the peace.

The Sixteenth District ceased to exist in 1936, one hundred years later, when all of the property became a part of the Great Smoky Mountains National Park.

For a while the Cades Cove area remained in the hands of a few grantees, such as William Tipton, the Calloways, and the Murray brothers, who claimed ownership to almost the entire watershed of the cove. But eventually the grant land was sold off — sometimes in an entire section, but more often the larger tracts were broken up. Through the years some individuals established sizable estates. For instance, D. D. Foute began to acquire mountain lands in the 1830s, and by 1856 he could advertise 15,000 acres for sale in the Cades Cove area alone; plus he held, either in sole ownership, or in partnership, close to 50,000 acres in the mountains surrounding the cove. By the late nineteenth century, however, most of the large estates had been divided and ownership dispersed, either by sale or by inheritance.

In the early part of this century, Morton Butler, a lumberman from Chicago, began rather quietly to buy up Cades Cove land that showed promise of timber production. Butler would buy the land through his agent, J. W. Post, and then deed it to the Morton Butler Lumber Company. He assembled some 25,000 acres under the ownership of his company, and was

Known today as the Elijah Oliver Cabin, this split level house was created by adding the kitchen section (once the home of the Herron family and located some distance away) to the main quarters.

The Tipton-Oliver House, like the farm buildings shown earlier, carries the names of the principal owners.

making plans to establish a sawmill in the cove when the National Park interfered.

Between 1928 and 1936 what was to be the final transfer of Cades Cove land occurred. The State of Tennessee purchased 105 parcels of land to be part of the Great Smoky Mountains National Park. Of these, only four were purchased from non-resident owners: the Morton Butler Lumber Company tract of 25,244 acres; two tracts owned by the Shea brothers totaling 696 acres, which had also been held for lumbering prospects; and a tract of 174 acres on Cades Cove Mountain, owned by a development company.

A total of 11,273 acres were held by resident owners. In exchange for their land they received a sum of $442,950.00, or about $39.00 per acre. This was considered a fair price at the time. Nevertheless, the debt we still owe these people for giving up their ancestral homes cannot be erased by the money paid to them. It is not possible to place a monetary value on what the people of Cades Cove and other areas of the Smokies had to sacrifice so that we can now enjoy a national park on this land. In this final transfer of property, a way of life disappeared from these valleys that can never be recaptured. We must preserve some understanding of this life, and, I hope, an appreciation of the sacrifices of these people, who, even if under protest, gave up their lands for the sake of society and its national park concepts. (See Appendix B for the land sales report.)

Varying numbers of people came to make their homes in Cades Cove during the life of the community. Population data are available from census records for 1830 through 1880 and from a 1917 mail list. It is difficult to determine the boundaries of the census accounts of 1830 and 1840, for in those years data were recorded in the order of the taker's visits from community to community, without naming the area. However, beginning with a name that can be placed in the Sixteenth District through other references and ending with another such name, we can assume that all names between were also in Cades Cove at the time the census was taken. There is bound to be some error in analyzing the records in this way, but it does give an indication of the population at these intervals.

There was a remarkable growth in the population of Cades Cove between 1821, when records first show that families were moving into the area, and 1850. The census of 1830 lists 44 households and a total population of 271. During this period the only access to the cove was by way of the old Indian traces. The area was not accessible from North Carolina due to the Indian situation at that time, and almost, if not all, of the settlers entered from Tuckaleechee Cove.

During the decade 1830-1840, five roads were opened into the cove, and the Cherokees were cleared from the area to the south. Several families, such as the Burchfield and the Sparks, came into Cades Cove from western North Carolina. By 1840 the population had swollen to 451 in 70 households.

The increase continued even more rapidly, and by 1850 the population was almost unbelievable — 685 in 132 households. It was impossible for the valley to sustain so many for long, since subsistence farming was the only source of support or food. A crash was inevitable, and by 1860 there remained only 45 households with 275 individuals, a return to the 1830 level. During the decade 1850-1860, a few new names were added to those already well established. The Whiteheads entered for the first time, as did the Powells and the Ledbetters. The Dunns came and left, finally settling in Tuckaleechee Cove. Most of the families who were there in 1850 and were not there in 1840

Known today as the Peter Cable House, this was actually built by Dan Lawson in the 1850s.

were also absent in 1860. It would appear that many of them were just on the way to somewhere and stopped over in Cades Cove for the census!

There was a gradual increase in population in 1870 (373) and 1880 (448). Some new names added during this period were Wilcox, Wilson, Sands, Proctor, Potter, Myers, LeQuire, Gregg, and Abbott. The population peaked a second time around 1900, 125 families, 708 individuals. A mail carrier's record of 1917, listing all occupants of the cove, records 116 families with a population of 540. Shortly after, families began leaving the cove, many because of employment possibilities at the Aluminum Company of America in Alcoa and at its power dam construction sites in North Carolina.

When land sales for the National Park began in 1928, many families moved out immediately. Only a few chose to remain on their homesites when the privilege was offered them. The few families still living in Cades Cove are leasees of the National Park Service, raising horses and cattle to maintain the open meadow nature of the valley.

Of the forty-four families in Cades Cove in 1830, only thirteen were still there in 1840. Only four of these thirteen were

A 1920s view of Spence Field Cabin, a hunter's and herder's cabin built by Tom Sparks. Sparks was murdered here in 1926.

there in 1850. The Tiptons left in the 1840s but returned in the 1850s for the rest of the life of the cove. Only two families, the Shields and the Oliver, were actually there throughout the life of the cove. Some families — Burchfield, Sparks, Anthony, and Gregory — entered in the 1830s and persisted.

The settlers of Cades Cove came — and went — over roads that were rugged and crude but that tied the secluded valley to the outlands throughout its history. The original roads, if they can be called such, were Indian trails. These pathways had served the Cherokees as access through Cades, Tuckaleechee, and Wear's coves to the settlements of the Holston Valley to the northeast. They were trade routes as well as warpaths. There were three of these well-worn paths. One came from the Little Tennessee River of western North Carolina, across the Great Smoky Divide at Ekaneetlee Gap. It followed the Ekaneetlee Branch to what is now Forge Creek to intersect in the cove with another path from the Indian villages on the Little Tennessee at Chilhowee and nearby. From these two paths, exit from the cove was made by a trail almost straight across the Cades Cove Mountain to Rich Gap and thence to Tuckaleechee Cove. This trail left the cove just to the east of where the Missionary Baptist Church now stands. The earliest settlers in Cades Cove entered by way of this last trail. It was well-worn and seemed to be adequate enough for them to get their household goods into the cove and to communicate regularly with the residents of Tuckaleechee. The path is still visible and was used extensively early in this century by people of the cove seeking a short cut across the mountain.

During the 1830s two turnpikes, or toll roads, were built which influenced access to the cove. One of these, known in the records as Parson's Turnpike, was west of the cove, from about the mouth of Abrams Creek, along the route generally followed by the present U.S. 129, into North Carolina. The other turnpike was never completed. It was to cross the mountain into North Carolina at the Spence Field. This road was opened to the state line, passing up Dry Valley, through the present School House Gap, thence through the White Oak Sinks to Laurel Creek, then up Bote Mountain to the Spence Field. Dr. Isaac Anderson, first president of Maryville College, was in charge of construction of this road, and it is listed in some of the records as the Anderson Turnpike, or the McCampbell-Anderson Turnpike or Road.

In 1836 a road was constructed from Cades Cove via Crib Gap to intersect the Anderson Turnpike where it crossed Laurel Creek. This appears to be the first second-class, or wagon, road connecting the cove with Tuckaleechee. In 1838, the county court authorized the building of a road from Cades Cove to connect with the Parson's Turnpike, and Russell Gregory was named supervisor of the project. The present Parson's Branch Road generally follows this latter route.

While these roads were being opened, a new one across Cades Cove and Rich Mountain was also under construction. Exact dates are not available, but it was authorized by the county court in 1836, and Absolum Wiseman was appointed overseer. This road crossed the Cades Cove Mountain at Indian Grave Gap. The present Rich Gap Road was built by the state in the early 1920s to replace the old one which had served so well for nearly a century.

In the 1830-1840 period, two additional roads were opened to connect Cades Cove with the outside. One of these is now identified as "an early access road to Cades Cove from Maryville." It is known locally as the Cooper Road, or Joe

Not all of the homes in Cades Cove were log cabins. Here, Russell D. and Jane Whitehead Burchfield stand in front of their new home in 1920.

Road, for Joe Cooper who supervised its construction. This road was first laid out by D. D. Foute in the 1830s, and became the principal route to Maryville for Cades Cove residents. Another road, following the original Indian path, connected the cove to Happy Valley and is known as the Rabbit Creek Road. It enters at the Abrams Falls Parking Area in the western end of the cove.

During the 1830s and 1840s the residents of the east end of the cove used the Crib Gap Road to the Anderson Turnpike, while those of the west end used the cross mountain road for access to Tuckaleechee and the Cooper Road for access to Maryville. Roads within the cove were developed as needed. Far from being isolated, Cades Cove residents had access to neighboring communities and their county seat. The opening of these roads was probably responsible for the great influx of families during the 1840s which swelled the population to its maximum by 1850. These roads were important community assets, and one of the few government intrusions was the road requirement which called all able-bodied men to help repair the roads every spring and fall.

An aerial view of Cades Cove in 1936 shows the land cleared for farming. Forests have since reclaimed most of these sites.

Building a Mountain Culture: community life in cades cove

Over the trails and roads they came, carrying their few household goods, their tools, their Bibles, their seeds. They came to clear the forests and make their living from the loamy soil. They built sturdy cabins from the trees they felled and then built barns and corn cribs and fences. The earliest pioneers must have been a heterogeneous group, with many different motivations driving them westward. But as the more restless ones moved on, those who remained in Cades Cove became more cohesive, bound by a common manner of life. It was not an easy life in the small community. The people worked hard and enjoyed their pleasures when they could. How they lived and passed their days here is part of the Cades Cove story. It is part of the mountain culture that is gone forever.

HOMELIFE

Cades Cove was a prosperous valley and it would return a good living for those who used it well. Each family provided for its own needs. Separated from the main American marketplace, people here had little use for cash in the day-to-day life of the cove. They depended upon themselves and their neighbors for the food and few comforts they enjoyed. Each person in the family, young and old alike, shared in maintaining the household. Work was central to the family life of these mountain people. Leisure time was a premium to be cherished.

Newly married couples seldom removed themselves far from one or the other of the parent families. Getting started, or "leaving the roost," was not a sudden occasion, but a slow process of weaning. Many families actually established a "weaner" house on their property. The newly married were still needed to help on the farm, and they needed to gain experience in independent living and home management. As their own family got under way, they would take over part of the farm, or move onto land of their own purchase, or even go off to the outside for jobs. In the earlier years, in many instances, this meant heading west. Oklahoma, Texas, and other western

Barns were a vital part of the farm life of the cove. This 1936 photo of the Cassie Myer's barn shows a style that was more spacious than the common log buildings.

states, even as far as Washington, have residents descended from Cades Cove people.

It is difficult for us of a modern culture to understand that a family had to provide almost all of the food to support itself and its livestock. This meant that from spring planting through the last days of harvest, every member of the family was involved in this process in one way or another. As soon as a child was big enough, his chores were assigned. The girls as well as the boys were field workers, and most of them could handle a double shovel plow and fork hay right along with the young men. The lives and work of the family followed the cycle of the seasons and the workings of nature upon which they were dependent.

After a winter with only stored, dried, and canned vegetables and fruits, the fresh wild greens of the spring were a welcome change. These included the wild cresses of the fields, the "bear" lettuce of the mountain streams, the toothwort of the moist stream banks, and, most abundant of all, the wild leek, or ramp, of the northern slopes. Ramps thrived above 3,000 feet elevation, and the trip to the ramp patch each spring was an all day affair for many families. The date was usually a Saturday in late March or early April. They would pack a lunch — something that would go well with the fresh ramps — and each member of the family would carry a short-handled, well-worn hoe or some other digger and a flour sack. Once in the patch, which covered several acres on the slopes, they proceeded to dig until their sacks were filled with the aromatic, broad leaf, bulbous plants. Back at home, they placed the plants in the spring branch, or in some cool, moist place, to keep them fresh for a week or more. The plant would be eaten raw, killed with hot grease, chopped in a salad with other greens, cooked and creamed, or chopped and mixed with corn meal for a delightful "corn dodger." Monday morning at school it was obvious who had been in the ramp patch that weekend, for the garlic-like odor of the uncooked ramps lingers on the breath for several days.

The first harvests of the season began as the garden vegetables came in. There was usually a daily picking to be served at once, though not enough at this time of year to put up. During a lull in mid-summer, as the crops were "laid-by," berry picking became an almost daily chore. First the blackberries along

the fence rows and in old fields ripened. Blackberry picking was mostly done by the women and children. Buckets filled fast and were carried back to the kitchen for cooking and canning, and, of course, a great blackberry cobbler to celebrate the first day's harvest! The last of the crop was usually made into jam and jelly.

About as soon as the blackberries were gone, the blueberries were ripening on the piney south slopes of the surrounding ridges. These slopes were burned regularly, if not by lightning fires, then by someone seeing to it that the berry crop would be good. If the slopes were not burned every three to five years, the process of succession would gradually eliminate the berry shrubs and later the pines. Pruning by burning encouraged the young growth of the blueberries, which produced the most fruit. I can still remember my delight as a child in seeing the beautiful fire patterns on the ridges at night when the undergrowth on the slopes was being burned.

Buckets did not fill so fast with the blueberries as they did with blackberries, and the sun bears down on those south slopes, but these did not have to be processed within a few

Hay harvest was almost a summer-long job for the men.
At left, Floyd and Luther Abbott with a load of hay. Above,
Luther and Floyd are joined by John Abbott in hoeing corn.

hours as the blackberries did. Picking would continue for several days until many gallons had been collected. They would be canned in half-gallon glass jars to be served as fruit or made into pies throughout the winter months.

While the women and children were harvesting berries, the men folk were usually busy putting up hay. Hay was not bailed in the early years, but was stored in the barn lofts or stacked in the fields. These field stacks were made around a central high pole which prevented the wind from blowing them over. The art was to pack the hay well and top it off so it would shed rain. All the barns had sizable hay storage areas. From the loft, the hay was pushed down directly into the stall mangers for the livestock, usually horses or mules. Cattle were fed on the outside, or from a hay rack under the barn overhang.

The first main farm crop to be harvested was the wheat. This grain was sown in the late fall, sometimes grazed by cattle in the winter, then allowed to come to maturity in the spring. Almost every farm had a wheat field of five to fifteen acres, which all came into maturity about the same time. In the earlier years, this harvest was done mostly by hand tools. A scythe with a cradle attached was used in the cutting. A simple swing of the scythe would cut enough for a bundle. The cradle prevented the stems from falling to the ground and made collecting and tying easier. One person could do the job, but it went faster if a second person could collect and tie the bundles. A well coordinated team could cradle quite a few acres in a day. The bundles were stacked so as to keep the ripe heads off the ground in case there was rain before they could be hauled to the barn or be threshed. In later years, horsedrawn harvesters became available. Families went together to purchase this mechanical wonder, or a more prosperous farmer acquired one and rented it to his neighbors. The first mowers just cut and cradled the wheat, feeding the bundles to the side where they still had to be collected and tied by hand. Later, a tying mechanism was added. It was quite a sight to see this machine moving around the field, kicking out bundles of wheat.

Threshing the grain was done at first by flailing. This was done in a clean area and on a windy day, since the wind hastened removal of the chaff. To make flailing easier, the heads were usually removed from the plants, or the bundles were arranged so that only the heads were flailed. In later years, a mechanized thresher, pulled about and powered by a steam engine, was supplied by one farmer who, after threshing his own crop, traveled from farm to farm and for a fee threshed his neighbors' crops. It usually took about a day to do each crop. The threshing crew was made up of several men, those whose wheat was being threshed and others who traveled with the machine until the community crop was in the granary. At each farm, or set, the women gathered to prepare the noon meal. And what a meal it would be! You may still hear a mountain person use the expression "enough for a threshin'."

Following threshing, the straw was used to replenish the mattresses for all the beds. After a year's use, even with almost daily fluffing, the beds were pretty hard, and the slats underneath could be felt through the worn straw. All the old straw was dumped out and the bed tick was washed and dried and stuffed anew with the fresh straw. There is really no experience quite like crawling into bed atop a new-filled straw mattress. The pleasing smell of the fresh straw remained for several weeks.

As the summer progressed, field beans and peas came in.

The earlier beans were picked and prepared for drying or pickling in the pod. The later crop was permitted to mature; the seeds were hulled out and stored for soup beans. Field peas, clay, crowder, and whippoorwill, were harvested in a similar manner. Potatoes were dug and stored in a hay-lined pit in a corner of the garden. A mound of dirt covered the stored potatoes and was covered in turn with wooden boards to keep out the rain. Cabbages were similarly stored, as were carrots, parsnips, and apples. Onions were pulled up, tied in bundles, and hung in a sheltered place to dry before being stored.

The harvest of a wild crop of chestnuts, which was very important to turkeys, bears, and domesticated hogs, as well as to the people, began early in September in the higher elevations and continued well into October. The nuts were gathered as they fell from the trees. It was no chore for a family to fill several bushel bags in a day. The crop was generally taken to market for the purchase of shoes and other items for which cash was needed. John McCaulley recalls that he and his two daughters went to the mountains near Gregory Bald and in one afternoon harvested seven bushels of chestnuts. He hauled them to Knoxville where he received $2.00 a bushel. This was enough in those days to buy all his six children shoes for the winter. Large quantities of the nuts were also consumed in the

The John P. Cable mill was one of several grist mills operating in the cove. Water-powered mills were an important community asset. The early family "tub" mills gave way to mills with powerful water wheels.

home. Pleasant memories of roasting chestnuts in the hot ashes of the fireplace still remain for those of us fortunate enough to have grown up in Cades Cove. One use of the nuts was to fatten the hogs before killing them for the winter's meat supply. This was usually done by simply taking the animals to the chestnut stands and leaving them for several weeks. They would not stray far, for much food was readily available. The flavor of chestnut-fattened porkers rivals that of the renowned Virginia hams which come from hogs "topped off" with Piedmont peanuts.

Corn harvest began as soon as the frost had killed the plants. On most farms, it began by topping and fodder pulling, which meant that the stalk was cut just above the ear and the tops stacked on end and tied into a large bundle. The stack was formed around a stalk to prevent the whole thing from tumbling over. The leaves below the ear were stripped off and tied into bundles, using a corn leaf to make the tie, and these bundles were placed on top of the stack. The tops and fodder were used as dry feed for cattle and horses. The ears could be left on the stalk until they had completely dried out. Then the corn ears were pulled from the stalk and tossed into the bed of a wagon or sled that was hauled through the field. From there the ears were pitched into a corn crib made especially for corn in the husk, with log or slatted board walls to permit air circulation.

From the very beginning, corn and wheat were the staple grain crops in Cades Cove and the other valleys of the southern Appalachians. Oats and rye were also grown. Oats were used as livestock feed. The rye was usually hauled to market, but occasionally it was ground for bread. The wheat was also ground for use in baking. Of them all, however, corn was the most important grain crop. It was the principal grain for feeding livestock, especially for fattening the hogs, but it was an important food for the people as well. It was used for bread and hominy, and, of course, was eaten fresh directly from the ear as soon as it matured. Most families served corn bread for two meals a day. Wheat bread was the choice for breakfast, but when the flour gave out toward spring, corn bread was the only one available for all three meals.

The use of corn, and occasionally wheat and rye, for manufacturing moonshine spirits should not be overlooked. When government-licensed distilleries existed in the cove, corn whiskey was the principal product. Even after Tennessee went dry in 1876, corn whiskey continued to be produced, but at a much greater effort. The grain was sprouted by soaking a large sackful in a stream. It was then allowed to dry before being ground into a coarse meal. The meal was placed in a wooden tub or barrel to which sugar and water were added. After fermentation, the product, called beer, was distilled.

With grain crops so important to life in the cove, mills to prepare the grains were an early necessity. The first were probably simple tub mills. The tub mill operates from the weight of a column of water or from the velocity of a directed stream striking a fly-wheel attached to the bottom of a shaft. Its drive shaft is vertical, in contrast to mills having overshot or undershot wheels, both operated by horizontal drive shafts. The overshot wheel operates wholly by gravity, with water filling buckets from the top. The undershot wheel depends upon water velocity striking the wheel blades at the bottom. Around 1831 Robert Shields and David Emmett built a mill with a large overshot wheel and installed equipment with separate rocks for grinding both corn and wheat. The wheat flour was further refined by silk screening (bolting) to remove the bran, thus making white bread possible. The Shields and Emmett mill rocks for grinding corn were very large and were geared to turn out several bushels of cornmeal per day. This was not the only overshot wheel-powered grist mill in the cove. George Rowan built one on Rowans Creek prior to the Civil War and it operated well into this century. The John P. Cable Mill was built in 1868. Henry Shields built and operated a mill powered by an undershot wheel on Anthony Creek, just below the present picnic area.

After flour mills were established, on Little River for example, the wheat was hauled to these mills and exchanged for flour. This was quicker and more practical than the cruder methods used in the cove. Corn, however, continued to be prepared at the cove mills.

Corn was not an important marketable product, for it could be consumed within the cove. Farmers having more than they needed for personal use, would sell or trade it to neighbors who came up short, and occasionally corn would be used in barter at the local store.

October brought the last of the apple harvest, another important product of the cove. There were no fruit trees there when the first settlers arrived at Cades Cove in the 1820s, as Abraham Jobe recalls, and they got their fruit from families in Tuckaleechee Cove. However, apple, peach, and plum trees were soon introduced, and by the latter part of the 1800s extensive orchards were in production throughout the cove. Every farm had a great variety of apple trees, with fruit ripening from June to October. George Powell probably had the largest orchard of both apples and peaches. He turned the fruit into brandy. Before Tennessee went dry, Powell operated a bonded distillery, well known for its fine quality whiskeys and brandies.

Apples were a source of cash for buying winter clothes, as well as for paying the taxes. They were hauled by wagon to Maryville and Knoxville to be sold on the market or peddled from house to house. Many bushels were retained for home use, to be processed into apple butter and jelly, canned, or stored for fresh fruit through the winter.

The harvest of the crops usually continued to late November. Then it was hog killing time. The first nights of freezing weather initiated this job of preparing the meat for winter meals. Sometimes neighbors got together for the big task, and it involved all but the smallest children of the family.

John Burchfield, Charlie Myers and
son, P. A., prepare a winter's supply
of pork. The hog-killing process involved
the entire family and sometimes
the neighbors too.

The kill was made by either shooting or striking the hog with a large sledgehammer between the eyes. A knife was inserted into the large artery at the heart to empty the blood from the body rapidly. This cleared the blood from the tissues and was done to all animals slaughtered for eating.

Several kettles of boiling water had to be ready, depending on the number of hogs being killed. It was usually the job of the older children to fill the kettles with water from the spring or creek and to keep the fires under them well stoked. As soon as the water was boiling, it was transferred to a large wooden vat, and immediately the dead animal was dunked into the hot water. When the hair had loosened, the hog was suspended from a rack by passing a stick through the hind legs, just behind the large tendons above the hoofs.

While the hog was suspended head down from the rack, the hair was scraped from the carcass with large knives. The abdomen was opened and all the insides were removed. These were dumped into tubs and turned over to the women folk, who cut all of the fat away from the intestines, separated the other organs, and prepared a meal of fresh liver for the family and neighbors. The intestines were cleaned out and, along with all the fat trimmings, were placed into a large kettle to have the fat rendered from them. After settling and cooling, the lard, as hog fat is called, was placed in cans for use in cooking. Cracklings, the remains from the lard rendering process, were used to flavor many dishes, including corn bread — called cracklin' bread in Cades Cove. It was a rich but delicious bread, especially if the cracklings were crisp.

Some of the hog fat was used to make the year's supply of soap. Lye for this process was supplied by leaching wood ashes. Every household had an ash hopper where ashes from the fireplace and kitchen stove were stored and covered to keep out the rain. At soap making time, water was poured into the hopper and the leachate collected below. This was passed through the ashes several times, finally resulting in a concentrate of fairly strong alkali. This lye was mixed in proper proportions with the fat in the kettle and the day-long process of cooking down began. When the cooking was done, the fire was pulled and the kettle covered. By the next day the soap had hardened enough to be cut into pieces. These were placed on boards to harden further before being stacked for storage. Oc-

Hunting was another important means of providing meat for the table. Millard McCaulley is shown with his hunting partner, c. 1920.

casionally the mixture would not harden, and it was put into ceramic crocks to be used as a semi-liquid soap. In either state it was an efficient cleanser for clothes, hands, or wooden floors.

The hog carcasses were hung overnight in the cold, to speed the loss of body heat and firm the flesh for easier carving. The following day, the carcass was cut and trimmed. Hams and shoulders were trimmed out for special curing, as were most of the sides. The backbone area was prepared as loins for roasting, for porkchops, or for stew meat. All lean trimmings were processed into sausage. The sausage was sometimes canned,

Women in the cove kept busy with household chores and child-rearing. Here, Kate Shields on washday. At right, Mayme McCaulley Tipton and daughter, Juanita.

but usually it was eaten while the bacon and hams were curing. The curing process usually meant packing the pork in salt for several weeks, then cleaning and smoking it for several days, then taking it down and packing it with a salt, brown sugar or molasses, and black pepper mixture. After a few weeks, the cut of meat could be hung in a dry area until needed. There were several variations in the curing process practiced in the cove, but all resulted in flavorful meat for the table.

At hog killing time the children acquired the nearest thing to a balloon they had in those days. The urinary bladders of the hogs were cleaned, blown up, and tied. After a few days of drying they made fine balloons, and ones not likely to burst easily. In fact, they served as basketballs and kicking balls, and would last for many hours of play.

There were other chores to be done to maintain the household besides those of providing food. The men had to make and repair the farm buildings and tools and cut trees for firewood. Women had to make cloth and clothing, do laundry and cleaning. I remember especially the spring floor-scrubbing that involved the women and children of the family. On one of the first warm sunny days of spring, all furniture was removed from the rooms of the house, kettles of hot water were prepared, scrub brooms rounded up, and the floors doused with hot water. Soap and "elbow grease" were applied to produce eat-off-of clean floors. When the floors were dry, the furniture was cleaned and replaced. Memories of the smell of a freshly

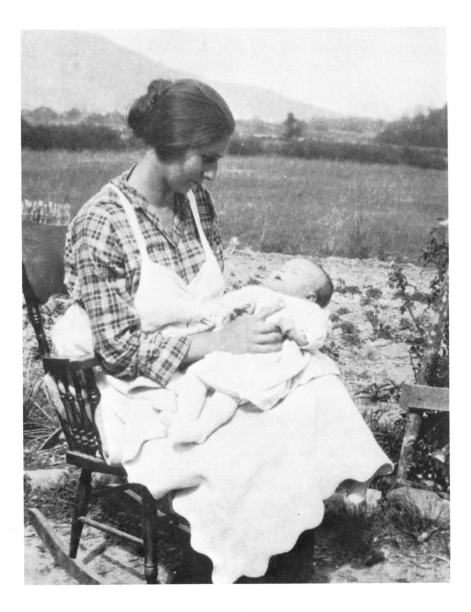

Children helped with the housekeeping, too. Here, in a 1936 photo, bedding is being aired at the J. M. Saults house, lived in that year by the Carson Tipton family.

scrubbed house far outweigh those of carrying the many gallons of water needed to do the job.

Providing firewood was an essential part of the homelife of every family, not only for heating water for special processes like canning and slaughtering, but for everyday use. Homes were heated with woodburning fireplaces and food was prepared with wood-fired stoves. The firewood was cut from whatever deciduous trees were available. Most farms had a section of forest reserved as the wood lot, to be cut for this purpose. The best firewood was hickory; oaks were next best. Hickory, the denser wood, burned more slowly and produced more heat. If there was not enough hickory available for all the wood, it was selected for back-sticks. A back-stick was a fire log placed at the back of the fireplace to force the burning logs toward the front and aid in reflecting heat to the room. A good hickory back-stick would last several days. The "dogs" supporting the burning logs were placed in front of the back log. Generally, trees were felled and cut into firewood as needed. The wood was burned before drying out, for if stacked and allowed to dry, it would burn too rapidly.

Cook stove wood was usually cut from pine trees. If the tree were dead, it would make the better cooking fire. If alive, the tree was cut and the wood split into small sticks and stacked to dry before being used. Quick heating was essential for meal preparation. However, for long periods of keeping the stove hot, such as for jelly making, slower burning wood was used.

The open fireplace was used exclusively for cooking in the early years. In winter it was used for preparing foods that required several hours of cooking. Pot hangers were installed in most of the fireplaces, and the Dutch oven was kept handy for breads, stews, etc. Potatoes were baked in the hot ashes almost daily throughout the winter months. The fireplace eventually gave way to the cook stove in the early nineteenth century. Stoves were manufactured as nearby as Knoxville and were probably the first items of furniture to be imported into the cove.

When schools were in session, the children had few morning chores, since they were usually leaving home quite early. A school day was from 8 a.m. to 4 p.m., and those who had to walk several miles left home early and returned home late. The usual evening chores were to stack the wood pile beside the front door and to fill the stove box in the kitchen. This would place the fuel handy for getting the breakfast and warming the front room. The front room was quite important in the winter, for the bedrooms were not heated. After the evening meal, the family gathered around the fireplace, where those in school did their homework, and the women did the mending and knitting. In some instances the father read to the family. In almost all cases, it was early to bed, for rising was also early. The fire was usually banked for the night.

The father was first to rise, build up the fire in winter, and get the kitchen stove fire going. He then went to the barn and fed the livestock. Meanwhile, the mother was busy with breakfast, grinding the coffee, making biscuits (if wheat flour were

Older children helped look after the younger while their parents worked or visited. Here, the children of John and Laura Cable Tipton.

available), cooking the meat. The children were usually called out as the bread went into the oven. Breakfast was a hearty meal.

School lunches were then packed into an oak-split basket or a large bucket, depending upon the number of children. Lunch consisted of whatever was available, meat and bread, vegetables, baked potatoes, or whatever. Schools were usually in session by early August and at that time of year there was always boiled corn-on-the-cob and large juicy tomatoes in the lunch basket. Lunch time at school would look like a picnic, especially if the weather were nice enough for eating outside. Each family group would assemble around the basket to be served by the oldest.

Weekends, especially Sundays, were days when only the essential things, like feeding the livestock and getting wood, were done. On Sunday mornings those families belonging to a church that supported a Sunday School were off on foot or by wagon by 8 or 9 o'clock, depending on the distance. Sunday afternoons, the children were usually free of chores and could visit with neighboring children to play. Whole families often visited on Sundays. The older folks exchanged news and gossip, and the young folks played games.

Life was not all hard work with no play in Cades Cove. There were special social times, in addition to Sunday neighborly visits, when people in the community joined together to share fun and fellowship. Many of these social events were associated with seasonal work, mostly with the harvest. Among these were berry stemming, bean stringing, apple peeling, and corn husking or shelling. Molasses-making time was also a time when families would gather around the local "'lasses mill" and help each other manufacture the staple sweet.

Berry stemmings occurred in late August or early September when the "gooseberries," sometimes called deerberries and related to the blueberries, were harvested. The berries were produced on fairly large bushes scattered over the foothills around Cades Cove. When ripe, they fell from the bush with their rather long stems intact. The harvesters shook the bush and the ripe berries fell onto a cloth placed underneath. Of course, berries already on the ground would have to be picked up one at a time. After the berries were harvested, the stems had to be removed before they could be prepared for canning or drying. Families and neighbors would cooperate in the stemming job, and all hands were called into action. When the job was finished, fresh apple cider (sometimes not so fresh) would be passed around, a banjo would appear, and a social hour ended the evening. The next evening, the same ritual would be repeated at another home. Sometimes several families pooled the harvest and completed the job for everyone in one evening. While stemming berries, friends passed around stories and community gossip. After all, there were no daily newspapers nor radio or television in those days.

Bean stringing (actually destringing) was usually another of the harvest events. Many bushels of beans were piled in a big heap in the center of the work area. Everyone dug in and pulled the fibrous strips from the beans, creating many small piles around the room or outside area. If the beans were to be dried, some of the group would string them whole on a long string, passing the large needle and string through the center of each bean pod. The batch of string beans would be about 10 or 12 feet long. These were hung up, usually on the front porch, to dry. When dehydrated, they were stored in cotton sacks until

Sundays were rest and fun days for Cades Cove families. Summer Sundays, like this one in 1924, often found youngsters cooling off in Tater Branch.

used. These were known as "leather britches" beans, and when rehydrated, cooked, and properly seasoned, they were delicious. Other beans would be broken, partially cooked, and packed in wooden barrels and salt pickled.

October was apple peeling time. Apple butter had to be made and apples canned and dried. This was often another time of neighborly cooperation and gossip exchange. Most families processed many bushels of apples. Some were sliced and put out in the sun on sheets to dry. This took a week or so, so someone was designated to look after the apple slices and rescue them if a shower came up, although rain was not common in October. Apple butter was made in the iron wash kettle or in a large copper kettle, and it was a hot job. The fire had to be maintained all day long. Someone had to stir the mix continuously with a long handled wooden paddle. Usually the older children took turns stirring. The thicker the batch became, the more efficient the stirring had to be to keep the mixture from "booping" out of the kettle.

Corn huskings and shellings could come most any time following harvest. An event associated with this occasion added extra fun. At a husking, any young man finding a red ear of corn could kiss the lady of his choice. This kept expectation high. Red ears were not too common, but most piles of corn would have a few.

Not all social occasions associated with the home were harvest events. Weddings were, of course, happy times in Cades Cove as elsewhere. Most of these were at the bride's home. The church was not used for these events, perhaps because, in many instances, "happy juice" was passed around, and this could not be done at a church. The first night following a wedding, not too uncommonly the groom's male friends raided the home, removed the groom and paraded him around the house on a fence rail.

There were also social events at holiday times. For instance, Christmas eve was marked by a peculiar type of socializing. Many of the young men, and occasionally young women as well, would gang up on horseback or afoot and go from house to house serenading. This consisted of parading around the house several times, shooting guns, ringing cowbells, and yelling loudly. The custom was for the host to come out after a few minutes and share a bit of liquid Christmas joy with the group. They would then proceed to the next house. The serenaders could be heard coming at great distances. By midnight many of them had to be put to bed, or in the nearest hayloft, to sleep off the effects of the shared "joy."

Most people who look back on family life in Cades Cove, even those who can remember seventy-five years, or further still as they recount the memories of their parents, do so with fondness of good fellowship and joy in sharing hardships as well as good times. They were busy with the chores of making a living, but life was bountiful and happy. Although there were rarely the luxuries of more than was necessary, very few Cades Cove families went hungry; and somehow or other, shoes and warm clothing were on hand for cold weather each year.

RELIGION

It is understandable that a people so dependent upon the land and all nature for their livelihood would be a religious people. In the earlier years they must have worshipped in their homes, with the father of the household serving as minister. But as more families settled the cove, they began to join together in worship. One of the earliest symbols of community was the establishment of churches.

The inhabitants of the cove were basically Baptists and Methodists. In the later years the Church of the Latter Day Saints (Mormons) had a small following, primarily a single family, the Harmons, who were permitted to use one of the Methodist churches for services.

The Baptist Church was organized June 16, 1827, when "met the arm of the Wears Cove Church in Cades Cove and after prayer to God for his blessings proceeds to business 1st we choose Brother Richard Davis moderator and Brother William Davis clerk so dismist in order." (From the official minutes.) The church was admitted to the Tennessee Baptist Association in October, 1829.

The Cades Cove Baptists had their controversies over the years. People within a community had differences of opinion then as now. The first major controversy was in 1838 when thirteen members were dismissed over the question of support for missions. This resulted in the organization of the Missionary Baptist Church and the establishment of the Primitive Tennessee Association of Baptists. Another break came around 1910-1912, when the Primitive Baptist congregation divided over certain doctrines regarding the age of salvation, or accountability. Elder Andy Gregory and Elder William H. Oliver led the two factions. This split spread into most of the neighboring congregations, so that when one was referred to as a Primitive Baptist, it was common to add "Gregory" or "Oliver" to the designation. The "Olivers" held the age of twelve to be that of accountability, when salvation was possible. The "Gregorys" could not accept the fact that younger children could not be saved as well.

The Missionary Baptist Church began when the thirteen members dismissed from the original church met in May of 1839 for formal organization. The church remained small until 1846, when a number of additions were made. The Civil War caused cessation of meetings from October, 1862, until 1865, as it did the meetings of the Primitive Baptists. Following the war, the church reassembled and drew up a revised list of members.

One of the highlights in the history of the Missionary Baptist Church was in 1893 when the then great evangelist Thomas Sexton came to the cove and held a soul-stirring revival. "The

Missionary Baptist Church, built in 1915. This church organized in 1839 after a disagreement caused a small group to leave their parent church.

little church of 22 called Bro. J. M. Saults as pastor and the first Saturday he preached, the doors of the church were opened and 20 gave their hands as desiring to unite with the Church.'' At almost every service more joined, until the congregation could support a regular pastor one-fourth time. In 1894, a building for the church was constructed on Hyatt Hill; a new building was constructed at the present site in 1915. A Sunday School which started in 1898 persisted until the church closed its doors in 1944.

The history of the Methodists in Cades Cove is not so clearly outlined as that of the Baptists. They may have, as a congregation, predated the organization of the Baptist Church. There is evidence that the congregation was established as early as 1824, and Cades Cove is on the list of churches on the Little River Circuit in 1830.

The site of the Cades Cove Methodist Church has apparently remained about where it is today. The log building was used for school purposes shortly after the Civil War. It was not until 1910, however, that the property was owned by the church. In that year, William A. Feezell deeded it to the trustees for "Love for the Church of Christ and to promote the cause of Christianity." The first frame church building was constructed in 1902 by the Reverend John McCampbell of Tuckaleechee. He completed it in 115 days, hand planing the lumber, and earned $115 for the job.

Shortly after the Civil War, the Methodist Church began breaking apart through the southland, and Cades Cove was not immune to the consequences. The ill feelings among the residents in the war's aftermath caused the little band of Methodists to draw apart. A group met in a schoolhouse across the loop road from the entrance to the Pine Oak Nature Trail and organized as the Hopewell Methodist Church. Later D. B. Lawson gave a half acre of land and assisted in the construction of a building. This was locally known as "Lawson's Church," and the associated cemetery became the Lawson family burial plot. This site is located on the crest of the hill just east of the Peter Cable Place. Lawson deeded the land to "God Almighty," a complication, to say the least, for government efforts to acquire the land for the park.

Each of the churches had a cemetery associated with it, for they served their members in death as well as life. The Primitive Baptist Cemetery is perhaps the oldest of the church burial places in Cades Cove. The pioneer settlers, such as the Olivers, Cables, and Shieldses, are buried there. There are about 230 graves there now, and family burials are still permitted. In a special use permit for this property that will expire in 1979, the people of the church have the right to use the premises for religious, memorial, and burial services; to maintain the building and grounds; and the right to remove and replace markers. (Primitive Baptist Cemetery and Church, photo p. 17).

The Methodist Church Cemetery is probably the second oldest church burial plot. The early settlers Tiptons, Feezells, and Sparkses are among the 80 marked graves there. Missionary Baptist Cemetery is the newest of the church cemeteries and has about 40 graves. The trustees reserve the right to hold religious services in the building. The cemetery is still open for burial to holders of plots within the enclosed area.

These church-associated cemeteries are among fourteen known burial plots in the Cades Cove area. As of 1970, an estimated 475 graves could be accounted for in the various plots. An exact number cannot be determined, however, because of the many unmarked graves. There are a few of these in each of the plots; and in the smaller ones, there are no markers at all.

In addition to the church cemeteries, several Cades Cove families had cemeteries near their homes. Some of these carry the name of the property where they are located, even though it is not known whether any or all of the graves are of that family. These private cemeteries include: the Cable Cemetery, developed by the John P. Cable family; the Burchfield Cemetery; "Graveyard Hill," of unknown origin; the Noah Burchfield Cemetery; the Davis Cemetery; the LeQuire Cemetery; the Post Cemetery; the Boring and Wilcox Cemetery; Brown's Hill (also known as Orebank Hill) Cemetery; and the Feezell Cemetery.

Whether a body was to be interred in a private or a church cemetery, the burial was usually a community affair. Undertaker service was practically unknown in Cades Cove before the 1920s. There were a few men adept at coffin making who would do the job without cost. In fact, a funeral was almost costless, except if cloth were purchased to line the casket.

Walnut trees were fairly plentiful and were most often used for the coffin. When a tree had to be cut, unless it was used for furniture, it was taken to a mill and sawed into boards which were then stored to be used for coffins. For many years Jim Cable sawed the boards on his water powered sash saw, and, if for coffins, at no cost.

When someone in Cades Cove died, a member of the family or a neighbor would go to the church where the interment would occur and ring the church bell. After several minutes of ringing and a short pause, the bell would toll the age of the deceased. The men, especially those who were near neighbors, would go from wherever they were working to the cemetery and start to open the grave. The coffin maker would be contacted; usually he was already on his way for boards if he did not have them on hand. Depending on the sex of the deceased, a neighbor man or woman would go to the home and properly

The Cades Cove Methodist Church was established as early as 1824 and remained on the same site throughout its history.

lay out the body, which had to be done before rigor mortis set in. The body was dressed in the burial clothes. Special dresses were made at the time for small girls, but usually a nice garment already on hand was used for others.

Wakes, or "sitting up" with the dead as it was known in the cove, were not elaborate events, but solemn occasions. Neighbors usually spelled each other in this chore. The body was laid out on a bed, in a back room if available, while the coffin was being made. Many houses had beds in the front room. The family sometimes slept at a neighbor house during this period. If it was summer, the "sitters" would usually remain on the front porch or in the yard. Occasionally one of the group would take a look at the body, as if to be assured all was well. Most of the food during this time was brought in by neighbors to relieve the family of this responsibility.

When the coffin was delivered to the home, neighbor ladies would pad and line it properly and the deceased would be placed in it. The casket was hauled to the cemetery for the funeral by a neighbor if the family did not have the proper conveyance. The casket would then be placed at the front of the church room and opened. Following the funeral sermon, the congregation would pass by to view the body. The lid was then replaced, usually with wood screws, and the casket carried into the cemetery for lowering by ropes into the grave, which may have been finished just moments before. Following the closing of the grave, the dirt would be formed into a mound and packed smooth with a spade. Neighbors then decorated the grave with paper flowers which some of the women folk had sat up all night making. If it was summer, wild or fresh garden flowers would be used.

After the funeral, field work or other activities would return to normal. At the most, only a couple of days had been lost. Of course, if the circumstances warranted, the bereaved family would be helped in any way needed.

Thus, the community shared in the events associated with a burial. Everyone knew that his turn might be next. In the summer, it was especially important to cooperate in burying the body as soon as possible, and the whole process was often completed within twenty-four hours of the ringing of the church bell. During epidemics, which took many lives in a short period of time, practically no work was accomplished other than digging graves and making coffins.

Oddly enough, there were few sudden deaths among the people of the cove. There were a few killings, but only a few. Death usually followed a sickness prolonged enough that when the church bell rang nearly everyone knew who had died. The tolling of the age sadly confirmed it.

Churches and their cemeteries were not always associated with solemn and sad occasions. They were also centers for some of the most important social activities for Cades Cove residents. Revival meetings, annual services of communion, and, for the Primitive Baptists, footwashing, were among the special religiously-oriented events. The footwashing was the occasion of all day services, usually for several days. It was similar to the Methodist Campground days, except the participants in the former went to their homes at night.

Revivals, mostly at the Missionary Baptist Church, were also times when families could assemble and exchange news and strengthen social ties. These were annual events in the evenings, usually in the autumn. Sometimes a traveling evangelist would be invited, but usually the regular pastor would be the preacher. The big event of all time in Cades Cove was apparently the revival held by the Rev. Thomas Sexton in 1893. When I was a child, people were still talking about this man. He was a dynamic speaker and used vivid stories to illustrate his message. He took his texts from events occurring during the meetings, to bring a sense of presence to the occasion. He must have had the whole cove worked into a religious fervor that was exceeded by nothing before or since.

In the later years, there was an all day program which involved grave decoration at the cemeteries and a program at each church. The audience traveled from church to church, pausing at noon for "dinner-on-the-grounds." The date was usually the last Sunday in May.

Decoration Day, as the event was called, was looked forward to for several months. Families would begin making artificial flowers from colored tissue paper as early as March. This was a spare time activity, and it would take many hours for the women folk to assure plenty of flowers to decorate the family graves. About a week prior to the big day, the men took tools to the cemeteries, cleaned away the last year's growth of vegetation, and remounded the graves. The week prior was a busy one in the homes. Baking of cakes and pies took place early in the week. Saturday was a mass cooking bee. The smell of frying chicken and roasting meats fairly pervaded the valley. The "Sunday-go-to-meetin'" clothes were readied.

On Sunday morning, loaded wagons and buggies and people on foot carrying armloads of paper flowers and baskets of food could be seen moving along the roads toward the churches. Most of them went directly to their respective family burial plots and placed the flowers on the newly remounded graves; then they proceeded to the first church program, which was usually the Missionary Baptist. There, a prepared program of songs and memorial speeches was presented. The speakers were selected from those who had a reputation for public speaking. There were quartets of local songsters, as well as groups invited from outside. From this church the crowd moved on to the Methodist Church, where the programs continued with participants who were related to people buried there. Then, on to the Primitive Baptist Church, but not until a two-hour layover at the grounds of the consolidated school for the most elaborate spread of food one can imagine. I can remember as a young lad how impressive those meals were. Youngsters vied with each other to see who could eat the most. Needless to say, the speakers at the Primitive Baptist Church performed to a lethargic audience in the afternoon!

Relatives came from great distances and this was really an occasion for visitation. Decoration Day was probably the biggest social event of the year for a long time, and it is still looked back upon fondly by the people who participated.

EDUCATION

The building of schools was another sign of a growing community, and the people who settled Cades Cove were as interested in educating their children as they were in providing places for worship. Sometimes the same building served both functions, such as the old log Methodist Church which was used as a school shortly after the Civil War.

In the 1820s, before the cove had its own schools, children were sent to Tuckaleechee Cove to board while going to school. Occasionally, however, someone would hold "old field" schools in Cades Cove. The teacher was usually a resident and was paid by the local patrons, as often in farm produce as in cash. An old field school was a simple log structure with a dirt floor and a fire pit in the center. A hole in the roof let out the smoke. There were a door and a few windows, which were glassless openings with shutters. The seats were arranged around the fire pit for warmth. Generally, school was in session on winter days when there was no work in the fields, or between crop tending and harvest.

By 1900, four one-room schools were operating in Cades Cove. Attendance at the schools varied, but in 1891 when John L. Law was the teacher of the Upper School, he had 80 pupils in a single room. Reading, writing, and arithmetic were about the only subjects taught. Law taught a 4½-month term for $22.50 per month. He paid $4 per month for room and board. Attendance reached as high as 120 in the one-room Lower School when the Reverend John McCampbell taught there in 1896-1897. All eight grades were taught by one person.

Rivalry was especially keen between the Lower and Upper Schools in baseball, spelling, speaking, and debate. It was not

Cable School was built in 1926 to serve the west end of the cove. It was the last school to operate in the cove, finally closing its doors in 1944.

unusual to see the entire population of the cove turn out for a baseball game between the two schools. When the schools consolidated, however, there simply was no one to compete with. The other two schools were small and had no facilities for baseball. A fine ballfield was developed at the consolidated school, and the game remained a favorite recess activity.

The Upper and the Lower Schools were consolidated in 1916 into a new building near the Primitive Baptist Church with the idea of developing a high school, but the high school failed to materialize. One by one the various schools closed. The last, the Cable School, closed its doors in 1944, and the children of families still remaining in the cove were transported by bus to the Townsend schools.

Families who wanted more education for their children than the schools of Cades Cove provided had to send them outside the cove. Prior to 1918, most of them, especially the young ladies, attended Porter Academy, which served the county youth for more than a century as a college preparatory and finishing school. Maryville College also operated a preparatory school. In 1901 C. W. ("Bill Joe") Henry opened a business school, which evolved by 1904 into a high school as well and came to be known as Maryville Polytechnic School. Several

Cades Cove young men and women attended this school. Maryville College was the institution for learning for many who went beyond high school. Some went to Johnson City Normal School (now East Tennessee University). A few of the young people returned to Cades Cove from college to teach those growing up in the cove after them.

The schools, like churches, were centers for social activities. The closing day, for instance, was participated in by all the families of children at the school. The afternoon was filled with pupil speeches, short plays, etc. Members of the community who were particularly talented would take part in the program, such as in ballad singing.

Throughout the school session, academically-oriented activities, such as debating and recitations, were popular events. Sometimes these took place in the evenings, and the school rooms were lighted by oil lamps hung on brackets on the side walls. Spelling bees were particularly integral to school and community life. Almost every Friday afternoon, the school benches would be shoved against opposite walls, the pupils divided into two groups, and a couple of hours would be spent spelling. A word was continued until spelled. The successful pupil would "turn down" those who had missed it. When one

Teaching school was not easy, with large classes and several grades sharing a single room. But, John W. Oliver seems to have his students under control for this 1901 photo.

progressed to the head of the line or side, he or she would cross over calling out the team number, "No. 1" or "No. 2." One student was designated tally keeper, and at the end of the period the team with the most crossovers would be declared the winners.

During the school year there were also community spelling bees in which all who wished could participate, and usually with an enthusiastic audience. My paternal grandmother, who could neither read nor write, was an excellent speller, and her fondest memories were of the many spelling bees of which she had been champion. She was a great help to me in my homework. If I could spell the word, she could correctly pronounce it; if I could correctly pronounce the word, she could spell it. It remained a game with her into her old age. She could not recognize the words in print, but at one time she could spell every word in the *Webster Blue Back Speller,* the common text book in her school days. She had very little formal schooling as a child, but her fondness for the spelling bees was shared by many in Cades Cove to whom school activities were associated with good times.

COMMUNICATION

Even though the people of Cades Cove were an independent lot, they enjoyed their occasional socials at the community churches and schools and in their homes. They also enjoyed knowing what was happening outside the cove. They were not so isolated in their mountain community as is sometimes thought, and while they probably did not spend a great deal of time thinking or talking about events outside — there was too much work to occupy their time — they were always eager to be in touch with what was going on.

One source of contact with the outside world was through the general store. Actually, an area the size of Cades Cove could support several stores, since storekeeping was not a person's full-time occupation. He was usually a farmer as well, and he would open the store to a customer who rang a bell or shouted to summon him from his fields.

We do not know exactly when the first general store was established in Cades Cove, or by whom. Daniel D. Foute operated a store after 1848 for a few years, but he may have taken it over from someone else. In the late 1800s and at the turn of the century, there were at least three general stores operating. The Leason Gregg-Cable-Saults-Hawkins-Burchfield store (1879 to about 1928) in the western end probably represents the longest continuity of any store in the cove. A store was located at the Tipton-Oliver place for several years, and other stores operated throughout the cove from time to time.

The earlier store buildings were of logs, seldom larger than about 15 feet by 30 feet, and had few windows. A woodburning stove was located near the center or toward the back. Since stores were not attended all day long, the stove fire was usually not maintained, except on the very coldest days. After saw mills came to the cove, the buildings were frame, but their size did not change much. The Burchfield and Gregory stores were the largest, about 20 feet by 40 feet, with a 14-foot ceiling. Shelves were behind a counter on one wall. The other wall and floor space in front of it were used for large hanging items and for barrels, boxes, and kegs. The counter was usually stacked with cloth bolts, candy jars, the plug tobacco cutter, scales for weighing out coffee, sugar, etc. A larger platform scale was on the floor for weighing bags of salt and other heavy items.

The storekeeper stocked what were usually classified as staples: bolt-cloth, horseshoes and nails, coffee, salt, and to-bacco. Tobacco included snuff, chewing, and smoking varieties, and cigarette paper was usually supplied along with the bagged "Bull Durham" and canned "Prince Albert." The latter was also smoked in pipes. Stick candy was a treat item usually kept in stock. Some medicines, such as salves, castor oil, epsom salts, and calomel, were also sold. Baking soda, baking powder, and at times lard or shortening were available, and some of the stores stocked flour as well. In later years, cheese, pork and beans, and soda crackers were kept in stock. The coffee was usually whole grain, but in the 1920s, ground coffee began to be handled in bulk. Sugar, both granulated and brown, and occasionally Karo syrup could be bought at the local store. "Octagon" soap for laundry and "Ivory" for the bath (for the ladies) were also stocked in the later years.

The larger stores carried sewing thread and needles, leather for shoes and harness repair, and harness hardware and shoe nails. Kerosene (coal oil), turpentine, and axle grease could

Although families in the cove were largely self-sufficient, there were some items they depended upon the stores and mail-order services to provide. The general stores were an important link between Cades Cove and the world outside.

also be obtained. School supplies were usually available. Slates, and later pencils and tablets, were sold at the store.

Barter was the principal method of trade, until the later years when the lumber companies in surrounding areas began to introduce a cash base to the cove economy. Chicken, eggs, butter, and furs were common items of barter, though sometimes grains, such as corn and wheat, were used. Labor was also traded. Since most of the storekeepers were also farmers, from time to time they needed extra help. It was not uncommon for the laborer to take his pay in store goods. It is interesting to see the variety of goods and methods of payment used in Cades Cove; Appendix C includes excerpts from a store record book.

Once or twice a month, the storekeeper hired, if there was not one in the family, a wagon and team, to haul the bartered items to Maryville or Knoxville and exchange them for his store goods and notions. In earlier days this was about a three-day venture. Two nights were usually spent on the road. They might make it to the livery stable in Maryville for the first night; then, after loading up the next day, the driver could make it back up Little River or well into the "Flats" for the second night; then back to the store on the third day. Trips to Knoxville markets may have taken even an extra day.

On these trips the storekeeper would gather news to pass on to his customers and bring back catalogs to show items he could special order for them. In the later years, families furnished their homes with manufactured furniture which they ordered through their local stores.

Sometimes a post office was associated with a store, even after Rural Free Delivery began. Everyone had to come to the post office for mail, so offering goods for sale was a sensible thing to do.

Postal service was, of course, one of the main ways for Cades Cove residents to communicate with others. Except for a few brief periods, there was a post office to receive and dispatch mail in Cades Cove from June 28, 1833, until October 31, 1947. For several of those years the post office alternated between William Feezell and Dan Lawson, apparently changing hands with the national elections.

Rural Free Delivery began in 1904, with John W. Oliver as the carrier. Prior to that date, everyone had to go to the post office to post or receive mail. When Oliver retired, in 1940,

Cades Cove residents were not so isolated as is sometimes supposed. The first automobile entered the cove on September 26, 1915. It was Jack Fisher's 1912 Cadillac, and he delighted the Witt Shields family with rides about the cove.

Murray T. Boring continued the R.F.D. for a year or two. He was then transferred to a Maryville, Tennessee, route, and the people remaining in the cove had to again visit the post office to send and receive their mail.

The earliest mail to Cades Cove was picked up at Chilhowee from a route (No. 3435) from Maryville to Conasauga. This route was 93 miles roundtrip, and was made once a week. It was let to G. Alexander for $700.00 per year. At Chilhowee, the mail to Cades Cove was picked up, along with that to Tuckaleechee Cove, Wear's Cove, Walden's Creek, and Sevierville, by a carrier who made the roundtrip in three days, a distance of 96 miles.

By 1858, the route had changed its origin to Sevierville, leaving at 6 a.m. on Wednesdays, via Henderson's Springs, Walden's Creek, Wear's Cove, and Tuckaleechee Cove, arriving at Cades Cove at 6 p.m., 39 miles one way. There is no note as to when the Chilhowee station was dropped from this route. It probably had something to do with the opening of a mail route from Knoxville to Sevierville, making that a more logical place to handle the mail to Cades Cove and the area in between; and it shortened the roundtrip route by about 18 miles, meaning a whole day's ride in those days.

After the Civil War, the mail source was changed from Sevierville back to Maryville. It was in the spring of 1866 that A. Seaton was awarded the contract for a route from Maryville to Ellijoy, via Gamble's Store, for the annual fee of $70.00. The highest bid was $624.00. In July of that year, the Maryville postmaster was directed to have the route extended to Cades Cove via Tuckaleechee Cove, but the contractor was not to be paid any additional fee for this. The contractor agreed, and on July 31, 1866, mail began from Maryville to Cades Cove once a week, a distance of 37 miles one way. By 1897 the schedule had been increased to three trips a week. A second post office, Cable, was established in Cades Cove on December 18, 1896, with Henry A. Saults as postmaster, but it was discontinued little more than a month later, perhaps being the shortest post office on record.

With the extension of the railroad into Tuckaleechee Cove, this became the new origin for mail to Cades Cove. From 1904 there were daily round trips from the cove, six days a week, Monday through Saturday. Inter-post office routes were known as "Star Routes" and the mail was carried in locked bags. After the Cades Cove post office was discontinued in 1947, the few residents remaining continued for a few years to receive their mail as a part of a Star Route out of Townsend (No. 27125). Now all of them have to go to the Townsend post office for their mail.

In the early 1890s, a telephone exchange was established in Tuckaleechee Cove, and in 1896 a line was extended into Cades Cove, offering still another source of communication with the outlands. The extension line was a private venture financed by four Cades Cove citizens, Calvin Gregory, Dan Lawson, Witt Shields, and Bud Gregory.

The phone lines at that time consisted of only a single wire strung from trees on insulators. Each phone had its own electrical source. Ringing the phone by turning the crank also powered the generator to create the current to transmit the ring impulse along the wire. A small battery transmitted the voice impulse. Anyone working on the line when the phone was ringing would receive quite a shock, though of harmless amperage. Jesse Brown still recalled in his ninety-seventh year his experience as a phone maintenance man on the Dan Lawson section of the line. He informed the household when he was to be working on the line and asked them not to ring the phone until he returned. Invariably one of the daughters, Catherine, would appear to forget and crank the phone, almost shocking him off the pole. When he returned, Catherine would appear sheepishly to be forgetful, but he was sure she was doing it on purpose.

Maintenance of the lines into the cove was expensive, and by 1904 the line across the mountain was abandoned. However, the connections between the homes were maintained for several years, and I can remember seeing the lines in the 1920s. Several Myers families in the northwestern section in the Tater Branch area connected their homes by phone and had a ready method of communication.

When the connection was intact to Tuckaleechee Cove, the phone was used mostly for emergency calls for medical aid, especially during the periods when there was no resident physician in the cove. It was also used by a few storekeepers to place orders for goods to be delivered at times when regular supply trips were not being made.

Cades Cove residents wanted others to know what was happening in the cove just as they wanted to learn news from elsewhere. The newspapers were another important means of communication, and the Blount County papers especially were avidly received and read. Correspondents from the cove sent items to the papers for publication. The charming columns of local news remain for us one of the most enlightening sources of information on Cades Cove life and people. These articles were written by people who were living the Cades Cove story, and I am including here, in the language of the time, several of the items as they appeared in county newspapers in the late 1800s and early 1900s.

MARYVILLE INDEX, September 18, 1878.

Deputy Elias Cooper on a recent raid in Chestnut Flats, Blount County, a few days since, accompanied by eight men, visited the isolated rum mill of George Powell where they seized 11 tubs of beer and mash, 4 tubs of pomice, 130 gallons of brandy singlings, 5 bushels of meal, 2 bushels of rye, 2 bushels of malt. The revenue squad also arrested Powell, the engineer of the mash mill, who subsequently escaped while the men and women of the household were abusing and threatening the officers. The captured property was destroyed. The officers, who immediately started for the city on foot, while passing an unfrequented place in the mountains, the squad was fired upon by parties in ambush — and a lively fusilade ensued. About 40 shots were fired by their assailants, the revenue squad returned the fire, but with what effect they were unable to ascertain. The attacking party remained in ambush. None of the revenue officers were wounded, though a bullet found its way through the clothing of Bennet Ledbetter with the revenue raiders.

MARYVILLE INDEX, December 4, 1878.

Cades Cove, November 26, 1878.

Editor of the Index: We learn with regret that the schools of this district will have to close in about two weeks due to lack of money. They are being taught by the Misses Tipton, daughters of Col. "Hamp" and is but justice to say that they have given almost entire satisfaction. This is Miss Lucy's first trial and right well has she discharged her duties. Miss Lizzie taught in the same house last year and her abilities as a teacher are too well known to need any comment. It is safe to say that they can get the schools again next year. Among the new arrivals in the Cove is Mr. White who is going to repair and run Squire Sparks' saw and grist mill. Mr. McCauley, a worker in iron also will be moving in and we are informed that he is an excellent workman. We gladly welcome such men to our neighborhood. They will supply a long needed want. Signed E. B. Desencroffer (?)

MARYVILLE TIMES, March 17, 1886.

Cades Cove News: Bad colds and inclement weather. We have heard of Whippoorwill Squalls, but have never heard of Post Office Squalls until the present. March 9th and

10th it was snowing and blowing snow 2 inches deep. Cannot think of turning ten post masters or rascals out and filling their places with true, well-tried democrats, as some folks call them. It is hard to tell what will happen under Democratic administration as many strange things have happened since they got in power. Times were harder than for twenty years and we believe and hope they will get better when the whole rascals are turned out of office. Peaches are thought to be killed by the cold. Apples are likely to be plenty, they do not often fail. Wheat crops look very unhealthy. It seems as though people cannot get their oats sowed on account of snow and rain. Not much corn land turned yet. About all we can get done is getting wood and feeding our stock for they are getting scarce and if winter lasts all spring, corn will be scarce also. Sorry to say that we, the people of the Cove, are not very interested in meetings or preaching or Sunday schools or anything else that is essential. Very little preaching done here lately. There is an appointment for Reverend Gulbirback, Methodist South, to preach at the Methodist church Saturday next. Reverend J. D. Lawson has an appointment to preach at the Baptist church in the Cove the third Sunday of March. He generally has an interested congregation in attendance on such occasions. Success for the Times with Talmage's son, a subscriber, March 10, 1886.

MARYVILLE TIMES, April 7, 1886.

Cades Cove News: I, Onetime, give you a few lines from the cove. Health is tolerably good at present. Farmers are getting along slowly for planting corn. Oats are coming up and are looking well. Wheat looks sickly, especially the old seed in the soil. Clover and red-topped grass are looking fine. Squire Lawson has the finest clover field, considering its size, than we have ever seen in the Cove. The Reverend B. A. Hill was appointed to preach in the Cove next Saturday and Sunday. We learned that Reverend William Boring contemplates organizing a Sunday School in the near future. Go ahead, brother Boring, we have been thinking a reformation should take place in the Cove as there has been little effort in that direction lately, except the moving of the Post Office. We understand there is great complaint by some of the Democratic friends on account of the post office being moved from where it was to a radical's, not a true well-tracked Democrat, as the Blount County citizens call him. It will be well enough if things come out alright if the newly appointed post master has operated Post Master General Bilas and all under him down to the Democratic Executive Committee of Blount County. I suppose some did not expect anything better from the present administration, but the best of men can be deceived sometimes. Move a little slower, Mr. Bilas, in making appointments it's likely to weaken the Democratic Party. We have abundance of rain for the last few days. Abrams Creek is higher than for several years. It is sweeping fences away, washing the soil off and damaging meadows, wheat and oats on the bottom lands. The creek is flowing low at ten A.M. Signed Teooter.

MARYVILLE TIMES, October 5, 1887.

How long will the 29th of September be remembered by the people of Maryville and Blount County? A question before the people that even the little boys and girls were interested in was decided. Maryville and Blount County stood by their reputation and rolled in a majority for the emendment. However, the vote from the 16th District was 13 for, 35 against. The total number of votes cast in Blount County for the amendment was 1611, against it 924. Total 2535. Blount County has 8,000 qualified voters.

[This was on an early vote for an amendment to the Constitution to prohibit the sale of alcoholic beverages.]

MARYVILLE TIMES, June 7, 1893.

Cades Cove News: Health of this place generally good. Farmers very busy in their crops which look promising. Miss Betty Walker of Tuckaleechee is quite low at Squire A. W. Shields' at this time. Mr. William Feezell and wife Mary were in Maryville a few days last week. E. L. Campbell and Dave Sparks went to Knoxville on a business trip last week. George Powell says that the cattle are doing better than common on Ole Smoky this spring. Mr. Alex Wilson who has been on the sick list is up and out at work again. John Bogle and James Wilson of Maryville was on the mountain with a party of men surveying land the past few days. W. T. McCaulley of Gamble's Store was in this place visiting last week. A number of people from Tuckaleechee were over at the close of the meeting. Rev. J. T. Sexton of Maryville closed a revival service here on May 28. He has labored hard and earnestly for the comission of many precious souls. The meeting lasted one week and there was 58 souls converted, and renewed and

Logging brought changes to the cove economy and lifestyle. Steam-powered sawmills, such as the one in Lawson's Sugarcove, shown below c. 1908, changed house structures from log to sawed lumber. At right, Sherman Myers shows a method of getting logs from the woods to the mill.

the various churches were greatly revived and strengthened. The people feel thankful to Bro. Sexton for the earnest work he did and as their appreciation of same gave him $20. May the Lord lead him to conquer and keep him humble in his sight is the wish of his many friends.

MARYVILLE TIMES, October 4, 1893, news item.
Killed their Man
On September 26, John Harvey Burchfield was killed at his home in the mountains near George Powell's. Theodore Rose and Will Burchfield, son of Sam, of the Flats, went to Harvey B's home and raised a quarrel over some old grudge when Rose pulled a revolver and shot once. Harvey then took Rose's pistol away from him, but Will B. who was standing near, gave Rose his revolver with which

he finished the job. Drs. Blankenship and Martin of this place reached there the next evening and found Burchfield shot in three places, once through the upper part of the lung, a little below the heart, and in his right arm, with a 38 caliber revolver. He died the next morning at 1 o'clock. A wife and three small children are left in destitute circumstances without any means of support. Both Rose and Will Burchfield had been drinking and were quarrelsome when they arrived at the home of Harvey Burchfield.

THE MARYVILLE RECORD, Friday, June 3, 1904.

A report is current that the Little River Lumber Co. is about to extend its line over the ridge into Cades Cove to provide an outlet for a lot of logs and lumber on the other side of the ridge. This would be a great thing for the people of the Cove, as it would get them within reach of an outside market, while now they cannot market their produce without a long haul over rough roads.

THE MARYVILLE RECORD, June 4, 1904.

News from Cades Cove: The Cove people go right on building houses. George Myers and W. M. Feezell and J.

T. Sparks have their houses completed. John MaGill has had his sawmill in the Cove for two weeks and has been batching but his wife came up and gave the place a turning over. The recent rains have refreshed the corn and the weeds so that the farmers can set their hats proper and take a harder hold of their plows and hoes to keep the corn from smothering the weeds. Mr. Sparks had porches put all around his house so that on a rainy day if his dogs get tired of looking in at one door they can trot around to another to look in without getting wet. Cades Cove is to have a physician of her own in a few days. That is not a bad thing as we have been forced to do without the luxury of being sick or wait a day or two after phoning for a doctor since the phone is to Townsend. The Cove had a prominent place in the marriage lisence column up to 1904. There being none but children left to wed the parents considered that it best to keep the names out of the column. Bot on second thought is Squire Burchfield and Miss Jane Whitehead who are almost grownups.

THE MARYVILLE RECORD, June 24, 1904.

Cades Cove News: We are expecting great flocks of people to come to the mountains in July. We had another rain Sunday. It still looks as if there may be more coming. Mack Shields would like to go the Worlds Fair but is afraid that they would want to ship him as culls. E. G. Oliver and John Oliver are cutting F. C. Spradlin's timber which will be logged to John MaGills sawmill. Some of our citizens seem to think that a medicine is no good unless it has whiskey in it. About a gallon to a spoonful of medicine. Everybody is anxiously looking forward to another wedding in our Cove soon as Dave Wilson goes to Millers Cove and gets back by Monday Morning. There is no telling how things are going to be run at Myers store now. We noticed a big book on the desk the other day and on the cover was the title "The Road to Success." It is currently rumored that Roddy Smith who once lived in this Cove was a caller here Sunday and the great question is did he call on her and did she greet him with a smile and say "How-de-do, sweetheart, come in." Noticed sometime ago that Dave Young of Maryville had sold out his store and was going to invest in a flying Jenney. Joseph McCauley has sold his store interest out to W. H. Myers and probably plans to go partners with Dave. Wish them much success. Maybe he intends to go into the mining business as that is looking up considerably in the Cove.

THE MARYVILLE RECORD, July 1, 1904.
Cades Cove News: Dr. MaGill is still busy with his patients. He reports that John Russells child cannot live much longer. John Anthony fell off a porch he was building for J. J. Gregory and broke his nose, but the doctor hopes to pull him through. Joseph McCauley neither invested in a flying jenney nor in a brass mine but went to Beecher and Posts lawyer so he is strawboss again. Charlie McCall was in the Cove Sat. and called on Jake Rose, requesting him to be in Knoxville next Monday. John MaGill was a witness against Rose. Since it has taken to raining so much J. T. Sparks said he is much pleased to have his porch all around, but his pleasure is as nothing beside that of his dogs. The Cove people are on a boom as to the rumor that the railroad is to invade the quiet realm of the Cove. Someone will be likely to start a hotel as the Cove will make one of the finest summer resorts with the added addition of the brass mine.

CADES COVE IN THE CIVIL WAR

As we can see in the newspaper items, the people of Cades Cove were not only interested in what was happening outside, they were sometimes divided in their opinions about those happenings. Families and neighbors frequently took opposite stands on issues of politics, religion, and prohibition. Perhaps this was most evident during the period of the Civil War, which tragically divided Cades Cove as it did the nation.

Cades Cove and the Great Smoky Mountains were not in the mainstream of the war, but they were nonetheless torn by the conflict. In general, those who lived in the eastern end of the cove were Union sympathizers while those of the western end sided with the Confederacy. Even though the state of Tennessee was officially Confederate, Rebel soldiers seemed to feel that the cove was fair game, for it was known to harbor Union sympathizers. The greater threat to the cove, however, was from bushwhackers or scavengers, renegade soldiers who favored no cause.

The men of East Tennessee who fought for the Union went to Kentucky to join their units. Company A, 3rd Tennessee

Cavalry, was largely composed of men from East Tennessee, especially from Blount and Sevier counties. George Washington (Carter) Shields, son of Henry Shields, was with B Company, 6th Infantry, and received a miniball in his hip at Shiloh which crippled him for life. Another son, David, died of measles while in the Union army, as did Walter Gregory. D. D. Foute had two sons in the Confederate army. At the close of the war, in January, 1865, the aging Foute was dragged from his sick bed in Cades Cove, hauled to Knoxville, and put in jail. His daughter begged for his release, and he was paroled to her, but under guard. He died that month at her home. In the settlement of Foute's estate after his death, there was a claim of indebtedness against his estate by John Rorex for $178.55. This was turned down because it ". . . was for the purchase of a horse to be ridden for the Confederacy by one O. B. Foute (son of D. D. Foute) in the cavalry service and is disallowed because it was an illegal operation."

There were a few skirmishes between wandering Confederate units, usually a company or fewer, and the Home Guard of Cades Cove and Tuckaleechee. Home Guard families placed their children at strategic spots, usually on trails entering the cove and along the ridge crests. The children would appear to be playing, building a playhouse or something, but if strangers passed, they would blow a hunting horn that could be heard throughout the cove. This warning gave time for the residents to prepare for whatever might result. Generally the intruders would be Rebel units looking for horses or food.

Sometimes, however, the intruders were Union soldiers who had escaped Southern prisons and were trying to return to Union lines. We know that they were helped along the way by sympathizers in Cades Cove, as recorded in the diary of one such prison escapee, a Lieutenant (later Major) Davis. Davis, along with several others, broke from Camp Sorgum in South Carolina on November 4, 1864. They reached the safety of a Union settlement in Knoxville by way of the Smokies and Cades Cove on December 5. A Mr. A. D. Welch led the party some of the way, as reported by Davis:

Dec. 1st. We had a good night's rest. Mr. Welch awoke us directly after daylight bringing out a good breakfast. We were soon on our way again. Mr. Welch piloted us over the mountains for about 10 miles, and then directed us so that we could not lose our way. We ate a lunch of corn bread and molasses. Mr. Welch gave us a good drink of apple brandy before eating. We traveled about 3 miles after bidding Mr. Welch good-bye and camped on the top of Smoky Mountain in a cabin. We had a hard day's march. Some of the mountains we had to climb were very steep, being a mile high from base to top.

Dec. 2nd. We arose about daybreak and again started on our trip. We had some hard climbing for an hour or so, but the descent soon commenced and continued until we reached Cades Cove. We entered the Cove about 3 p.m. and very un-expectedly caused quite an alarm. A girl was on duty as a sentinel. She gave the alarm with a horn. When she blew the horn we were looking down the Cove. In an instant it was alive. The men were driving their cattle before them and every man had a gun over his shoulder. We asked the girl to point out the home of Mr. Rowan after telling her who we were, assuring her that we were friends. We marched on and went to Mrs. Rowan's home. She was very much frightened when she saw us, but we soon satisfied her that we were friends. She informed us that they were looking for the Rebels every moment. Rather pleasant news for us. We had not more than got seated when a woman came running up the road to Mrs. Rowan and informed her that the Rebs were coming. We jumped up ready to run, but we soon found out that the woman had taken us for the Rebels, and that it was a false alarm. Mrs. Rowan said she could not keep all of us, so five of us started over to the home of Mr. Sparks to whom she directed us. We soon found out that our entrance had alarmed all of the inhabitants of the Cove. The men left the fields and fled to the mountains. It soon became known who we were. They commenced to collect around us. We were resting very comfortably at Mr. Spark's telling our story when a horseman came riding up from the lower end of the Cove and said "the Rebels are coming sure," that one of the citizens had seen them. All was confusion for some moments. The men picked up their guns and we our blankets and started for the mountains. We reached a safe place. After waiting for an hour, we found out that it was another false alarm. The report had gone down one side of the Cove and up the other. We all returned to Mr. Spark's house and ate a hearty supper. We found all good Union men here. They all have to sleep in the bushes every night, and have for the past two years. They live in continued terror of being killed. At dark we went to the bushes for our night's rest.

Dec. 3rd. Breakfasted with Mr. Haslet [?]. *Raining by spells all day. Citizens are trying to get horses to carry us to Knoxville tomorrow. Four of our party not being very foot sore, took the road for Tucasuge* [Tuckaleechee] *Cove, the balance went in search of horses. When we reached the top of the mountain, we sat down to wait for the rest of the party. While waiting we had a lunch of bear meat and corn bread. Getting wet and cold, concluded not to wait any longer. Left word on a tree that we had gone on to Tuckasuge Cove, where we arrived at 4 o'clock. We stopped at the house of a good Union man, Mr. McCampbell, the balance of the party arriving about dark without horses. Three of the party went to the home of Mr. Snider and stopped for the night. Mr. Welch* [not the same Welch who befriended them in North Carolina] *and Mr. Gregory are out this evening after our horses. This Cove is a "true blue settlement." It gave 146 votes for Lincoln. McLellan did not receive a vote. We had a very fine supper, plenty of good apples, spent a pleasant evening with old Grandfather McCampbell, 74 years of age, who kept us talking all the time. He was full of old Revolutionary stories. We are beginning to feel as if we were getting near home. Cleared up about sunset. Had a beautiful night, moon as bright as a new dollar. Slept in the corn crib and were very comfortable.*

Dec. 4th. Our friends woke us at daybreak with the salutation "Breakfast is ready." We soon got ready and sat down to a well filled table and ate to our heart's content. Messrs. Grant and Welch were unable to get horses for the whole trip, but got horses to carry us across the Little River, which we had to cross three times, got started about 10 a.m. forming quite a cavalcade. Messrs. Welch & Gregory are going to Knoxville with us to get ammunition for the citizens of Cades Cove. About one o'clock we reached the Allegheny River [Tennessee? Holston? French Broad?]. *After crossing we sat down and had lunch, sweet bread, pies and apples. Marched over thirty miles today. The road is in good condition. Passed an Indian settlement on the banks of Little River. Four of our party stopped at the house of Mr. John Brown 3½ miles to*

Knoxville, the balance of the party continued on to find another house to stop in for the night. After a great deal of trouble found one, the residence of Mr. Harmon who lived within 1½ miles of our picket lines. We had a beautiful day. The whole party is feeling very gay.

Dec. 5th Happy Day. Moved into the City of Knoxville.

Near the end of the war when the Union army was cleaning up the area with units in Knoxville and Maryville, the Confederates used the route through Cades Cove for escape. They usually followed the road through the "Flats of the Mountains," locally called the Joe Road, camped overnight in the cove, proceeded by way of the Trough Branch Road (Parson's Branch Road) to the toll road (U.S. 129), and from there into North Carolina and on to South Carolina. One such unit, said to consist of about 300 men, some on horseback, entered the cove by way of the old Joe Road on a December afternoon in 1864. The unit broke up into smaller groups and scattered out over the west end of the cove to encamp for the night. One group made camp near the spring and down the hollow a bit from the house of Russell Gregory, who was away from home when they arrived. Gregory returned home at dusk to find the army unit encamped just below his house and making supper of one of his calves. He fortified his courage a bit with the usual liquid, picked his rifle from over the door, and walked down the hill to demand payment for his yearling. The camp guard hardly hesitated when he saw the approach of a rifle-bearing native and proceeded to shoot Mr. Gregory, age 69.

Resentments and fears ran so hard during the war years that even efforts to hold religious services in the cove were abandoned between 1862 and mid-1865. The Tennessee Association minutes of the Cades Cove Baptist Church reflect this:

We the Primitive Baptist Church in Blount County in Cades Cove, do show to the public why we have not kept up our Church meeting. It was on account of the Rebellion and we was Union people and the Rebels was too strong here in Cades Cove. Our preacher was obliged to leave sometimes, and thank God we once more can meet, though it was from August, 1862, until June, 1865 that we did not meet.

Bitterness still persisted among neighbors for a decade or more after the war ended.

Making a Mark:
people of cades cove

Who were these people who settled and prospered here, who built their homes and schools and churches, who raised their children and buried their loved ones in the cove? The families who opened up Cades Cove were pioneering families who found here a virgin, fertile valley and reaped bountiful harvests of their labors. They were typical of the true pioneers, subsisting and prospering by their own ingenuity. Another type people would later come to the Southern Appalachians to exploit the environment for coal and timber, to be dependent upon company stores for subsistence, and to introduce a far different approach to life. But the people who first pioneered, who found their greenest pastures here and stayed, these are the people of this Cades Cove story. They clung proudly to what they owned, and they left their mark for the future.

THE census data through 1880 include more than 150 names of families who lived in the cove during its first 60 years as a community, and about a dozen new names were added between 1880 and 1920. Some of these families were never very large; some remained but a short time and then moved on. Not all of the families can be included in this story, but those who seemed to have had a particular influence on the development of the cove are given a place in these pages. After all, the community of Cades Cove was its people, and their individual and family contributions should not be overlooked. They are described here in no particular order but to show to some degree their respective impact upon the cove and the close relationships of many of them.

THE TIPTON FAMILY

The Tiptons have a long history in East Tennessee and played a significant role in the early history of the state. They were, perhaps, *the* family to open up Cades Cove. A Revolutionary War veteran, Colonel John Tipton, brought his family from Virginia to upper east Tennessee, near Jonesboro, in 1782. A son, William (Fightin' Billy) Tipton, himself a veteran of the Revolution, moved into Blount County, settling on Little River near what is now known as Lakemont. He consolidated some earlier North Carolina and Tennessee land grants in the Cades Cove area, and in 1821 he was issued a Tennessee grant for 640 acres in the eastern end of the cove. Other grants followed until he had ownership of most of the bottom of the valley. He began at once to sell this land to friends and relatives of Carter and Johnson counties of upper east Tennessee.

Two brothers of William Tipton were in Cades Cove near the beginning of the settlement. One, Benjamin, owned property near the Primitive Baptist Church, but sold and moved out in the 1830s. Another, Thomas, held ownership of a large tract of land in the cove and is listed in the 1830 census. One of his daughters was the wife of Joshua Jobe, who made the first purchase of land in the cove and moved there with his family in the fall of 1821. A son, Jacob, was killed by Indians while hunting game in the cove in the late 1820s.

Samuel and Mary N. (Sally) Abbott Tipton on their wedding day, August 19, 1905.

The Cades Cove Tiptons descended from two sons of William, Jacob T. and Jonathan R. Jacob T. bought his first land from his father in 1824 and added to it with later purchases. Jacob Tipton was a community leader, and a justice of peace for the district. His house was designated as the voting place when the Sixteenth Civil District was established. He was a bit "hot-headed," according to stories that have been handed down. He usually started fighting before asking questions, much to his own discomfiture at times. Abraham Jobe recalls in his memoirs an instance when Jacob attacked his father, Joshua Jobe, to be bested by a smaller man who did not hesitate to use rocks to defend himself. There is also a tale in the Shields family of Jacob Tipton and a son tangling with Robert Shields and a son. Tipton supposedly got the better of this encounter, but the Shields son swore to not roll down his sleeves until he had rendered Tipton a "lickin'." He never got the chance to try and lived to old age always wearing rolled up sleeves.

In 1848 Jacob Tipton disposed of most of his property and moved his entire family, including in-laws, to Missouri. One of Jacob's sons, John J. Tipton, married Charlotte Hollingsworth, and when she died a few years after the move to Missouri, he brought his children back to Blount County. All of the children except a son, Nathaniel Hampton, eventually returned to Missouri. Meanwhile, John J. married Naomi Abbott, a daughter of Absolum Abbott, and she bore him eight additional children. Most of the Tiptons remaining in Cades Cove by 1930 were descendants of this marriage. A son, John Franklin, was murdered by "Smoke" Sam Burchfield, in August of 1901, leaving his wife, Harriet Burchfield, and five sons. Another son, Grayson Ambrose (1868-1931) contributed the most to the Tipton population of Cades Cove and the surrounding area. He fathered ten children, and a son of his, Ambrose, contributed ten more.

There is no record that Jonathan R. Tipton ever actually lived in Cades Cove. He was married first to Margaret Watson, and one of their sons, Col. J. W. H. Tipton, bought land in Cades Cove, moved there after the Civil War, and built the Tipton-Oliver place. Jonathan R. later married Elizabeth Johnson, and two of their children left quite a few Cades Cove descendants.

THE OLIVER FAMILY

The exact date of the Olivers' arrival in Cades Cove is not clear. Members of the family claim that John and Lurany Frazier Oliver moved into the cove in 1818. If so, they were there illegally, since the area was Cherokee territory until the Calhoun Treaty in 1819. This, of course, was not unusual, for families were constantly pressing the Cherokees, and other Indians as well, by gradually invading their territories as fast as new lines were established. There is evidence to indicate that pioneer families had tried out the cove even as early as the 1790s.

John Oliver (1793-1863) came to Cades Cove from Carter County, Tennessee, as did the Tiptons, the Harts, the Jobes, and the Cables. He was a soldier of the War of 1812 and was at the Battle of the Horse Shoe. John bought his first land from Isaac Hart, a brother-in-law of William Tipton, in 1826, and later purchased additional land from Hart and from William Tipton.

Two daughters of John and Lurany married into the Shields

family. The sons, Elijah and William, were progenitors of the later Cades Cove Olivers.

THE SHIELDS FAMILY

About the time Col. John Tipton was migrating from Virginia to upper east Tennessee, another Revolutionary War veteran, Robert Shields, was bringing his family, in-laws and all, from Virginia to Sevier County, Tennessee. They built a fort at the base of what is now called Shields Mountain, near Pigeon Forge, because they were invading territory still contested by the Cherokee Indians. In 1793, one of the sons, Thomas, and the only son-in-law were killed by the Cherokees while watering horses outside the fort. The son-in-law was Joshua Tipton who had married the only daughter, Jennet. She and at least six of her brothers went to the frontier of Indiana in 1807. Her son, John Tipton, became a military and political leader of that state and served in the U.S. Senate from 1831 until his death in 1839.

One son of Robert, John, was a gunsmith and scout for the Lewis and Clark Expedition. An older son, Richard, was the father of Robert (1784-1850). This Robert married Margaret Emert (1781-1862) of Sevier County in 1812 and became the progenitor of the Cades Cove Shieldses. In 1819, after the signing of the Calhoun Treaty, the family, already with at least three children, moved to the valley of the Little Tennessee River near Chilhowee. Early in the 1820s, a typhoid epidemic broke out in that community and the family moved on to the headwaters of Forge Creek in the Cades Cove area. The spot they chose was an isolated Sugar Cove upstream from where the Gregory Ridge trail leaves the stream to ascend the ridge. Later they moved out into Cades Cove, first settling on property of William Tipton near what is now the Tipton-Oliver place.

In 1831, Robert purchased 1,600 acres of land from William Tipton. Along with several other men, he opened a bloomery forge to produce a low-grade iron, and with David Emmett he built the first overshot water-powered grist and flour mill in the cove. The mill continued to operate until about 1930. Robert Shields was elected justice of peace of the Sixteenth Civil District as soon as the district was established and served until his

Andrew Witt Shields, one of the leading landowners and citizens of Cades Cove.

death in 1850. One of his first acts as a member of the county court was to petition for a road from Tuckaleechee to Cades Cove. He was also active in the church and was a delegate to the Tennessee Baptist Association in the 1830s and 1840s.

Two sons of the eleven children of Robert and Margaret Emert Shields married daughters of John and Lurany Frazier Oliver and remained in Cades Cove. Frederick, my great-grandfather, married Mary (Polly) Oliver and occupied the Robert Shields homeplace, with the grist mill, in the western end of the valley. They reared eleven children to maturity. Henry H. Shields married Martha Oliver and reared five children in the eastern end of the valley. A son, Witt Shields, became a large land holder and community leader. He was postmaster and justice of peace for several years. He donated four acres of land for the consolidated school and piped water from his home supply to the school. He also built a large 2½-story frame house and piped water to the kitchen, which was a real innovation for the time and place. He was also known as an inventor in farming and built his own wheat harvester.

Descendants of the Frederick and Henry Shields families were residents of the cove when it became a portion of the National Park. Leasees Kermit Caughron and Hugh Myers, still residing in Cades Cove, are descended from Frederick Shields.

THE McCAULLEY FAMILY

James McCaulley was married to Unity Elizabeth Caldwell in 1860. In September, 1862, he, with several of his friends, hiked to Kentucky and joined the 3rd Regiment of the Tennessee Cavalry Volunteers, which he served as a blacksmith until he was mustered out in June, 1865. During this period the family lived near Walland, in Blount County. In 1878 he moved his family to Cades Cove where he set up a blacksmith and woodworking shop, serving the community in this capacity for over twenty-five years. He was a principal coffin maker and taught the art to his son, John, who made coffins until the late 1940s. John married Rutha Myers, and his family was in the cove through the 1930s. John was renowned as a wild turkey hunter. A daughter, Mary Jane, was the only other one of the McCaulley children to remain in Cades Cove. She married William H. Shields, a son of Frederick Shields, and they were my grandparents.

PETER CABLE

In June, 1825, Peter and Dan Cable purchased a tract of Cades Cove land from Jabez Thurman. They were brothers from Carter County, Tennessee. Dan Cable never lived in the cove, although he is listed again in 1836 as a co-buyer, with his brother, of the remainder of the Thurman property. Another brother, Samuel Cable, moved into the cove with his family along with Peter. In 1839, he moved across the mountain to the headwaters of Hazel Creek, giving rise to the community of Cable Cove.

Peter Cable (1792-1866) brought his wife, Catherine Hallows (1794-1848) to the cove, and the family is recorded in the 1830 census. There were three children, all born in Cades Cove prior to 1830.

Peter Cable was active in the community in the early years

of the settlement. He was a co-founder of the Primitive Baptist Church, and he and John Oliver were the agents who signed for the original gift of land to the church by William Tipton. His home was just west of the present "Peter Cable Place" and across the branch near a large white oak tree. He sold his property to this son-in-law, Daniel B. Lawson, in 1856. The deed was registered a month before his death in 1866.

Becky Cable at her spinning wheel, 1936. Aunt Becky managed a store, kept boarders, farmed her land, and cared for the orphaned children of her brother. She died in 1940 at age 96. Her house is exhibited as part of the Cable Mill Area in Cades Cove.

JOHN P. CABLE

John Primer Cable was a nephew of Peter Cable, the son of Benjamin. He was born in Carter County, Tennessee, in 1819. John married Elizabeth Whitehead, possibly also of Carter

County, and they brought their family to Cades Cove in 1867. There is no record of any children being born after that date. Cable purchased land in 1868 and in 1869 from G. W. Feezell. In 1882 he entered for a state grant to consolidate title to a small tract of land lying within the boundaries of his purchase. On this newly purchased land John P. Cable constructed a water-powered saw mill and a grist mill. He used the base of the old forge dam to impound Forge Creek and direct the water by a canal to his impoundment on Mill Creek, thereby obtaining ample water for his mills during the dry seasons. Later, in the 1880s, he purchased mountain land on Sugar Cove Branch, near Pole Knob.

John P. Cable is on lists associated with local churches and various committees. He was also involved in local politics, and, in general, was a leader in the community. A son, James V., inherited the mill complex and was a successful blacksmith, sawmiller, and farmer. He built a two-story sawed log house at Forge Creek, upstream from the mill, and it was a masterpiece of construction. It is a daughter, Rebecca (Aunt Becky), however, who is best remembered of the family.

In 1879, Leason Gregg bought one acre of land from John P. Cable, built a two-story frame house, most likely from lumber sawed at the Cable Mill, and opened a general store. This is thought to be the first frame house built in the cove, and is essentially the same one that is displayed as the "Becky Cable House" at the Cable Mill exhibit complex. The store and home were located upstream from the present site, on the right of the road leading to the Henry Whitehead place. The Gregg family lived on the second floor and used the first floor for the store. In 1887, Rebecca Cable and her brother, Dan, bought out Gregg, who moved to Friendsville, Tennessee. Dan Cable operated the store until 1896, when he sold it to J. M. Saults, who moved the goods to a new building. Dan was eventually committed to a state hospital and his wife died of tuberculosis, leaving Rebecca to care for the family. "Aunt Becky," as she was known to most of the younger generations, was a hardworking, astute manager, and was respected by all. She kept boarders, mostly saw mill workers, farmed her small acreage, grazed cattle on her father's mountain property, which she finally gained possession of, and bore the burden of caring for the children of her brother.

DANIEL B. LAWSON

Daniel Bird Lawson (1827-1905) was the son of Howell and Mary Bird Lawson of Greene County, Tennessee. The family moved to Blount County prior to 1850, although it is not clear whether they first moved to Wear's Cove or Tuckaleechee Cove. Dan went to work for Peter Cable in Cades Cove and married his older daughter, Mary Jane, in 1850.

Dan Lawson was an influential citizen of Cades Cove and Blount County. He was for a time the postmaster, and for several years a justice of peace. He added to his original purchase from Peter Cable, especially taking advantage of the public sales of the lands of D. D. Foute. Lawson eventually owned a strip of land running south to north across the center of the cove, from the state line to the crest of Cades Cove Mountain. He was active in the Methodist Church, serving as a trustee, and donated the land for the "Northern" Church after the Civil War. His property was divided among his five surviving children. Two had died young.

The present "Peter Cable Place" is a part of the Lawson home, probably the first portion constructed. From time to time frame additions were built as the family grew, until the final structure was a rambling style home.

THE ABBOTT FAMILY

The Cades Cove Abbotts began with Absolum, Sr. (1804-1878), a Baptist preacher who lived in the cove for twelve years. Absolum married Annis Stillwell (1805-1853) and they had five children. Three of their sons were in the Civil War.

Noah, father of the cove Abbotts, served with the H and E companies of the 9th Tennessee Cavalry as private and corporal. Noah and his wife, Nancy Hatcher, moved to Cades Cove in the 1870s. He is listed in the census of 1880 with eleven individuals in the household. Of the children of Noah Abbott, only John (1863-1925) remained in Cades Cove. He married Rhoda Lawson, a daughter of Dan Lawson. She inherited the Lawson homeplace where they reared a family of eight children, all but one of which married into cove families.

Noah Abbott, Civil War veteran and the first of the Cades Cove Abbotts.

THE BURCHFIELD FAMILY

The Burchfields of Cades Cove came from Yancy County, North Carolina, and it is a difficult family to untangle. It appears, from the census data, that there could have been at least four brothers involved: Robert, Moses Y., Nathan, and Wilson (Wilse). The 1840 census records list a Robert and a Moses Y. Burchfield. The families of these two are fairly clear. Moses Y. Burchfield is listed in the 1850 census but not thereafter, and his family probably left the cove in the exodus of the 1850s.

Robert Burchfield, the first to become established in Cades Cove, purchased 150 acres of land in the cove from Casper Cable in 1834. This was part of a Tennessee grant of 160 acres to Abraham Tipton. Tipton had sold the 150 acres to Cable in 1831, although neither Tipton nor Cable had resided in the cove. In 1835, Robert Burchfield bought the additional 10 acres directly from Abraham Tipton. Descendants of Robert were living in the cove and on the original land site at the time of purchase for the park. Robert Burchfield was first married to Elizabeth Hill, and fathered ten children. Upon her death in 1841, he married Mary Gregory, a daughter of Russell Gregory, and fathered seven additional children.

In 1850 there is on record a Nathan Burchfield and wife, Mary. The arrival of the Wilson (Wilse) Burchfield family to the cove cannot be pinpointed either, but we presume it was in the 1860s. The direct relationship of these to other Burchfields can only be surmised, but it was generally understood that all the Burchfields were related. In 1873, Wilson Burchfield purchased the George M. Shields grant in the Chestnut Flats. In 1884, he entered for 5,000 additional acres, which was the north slope of the Smokies, including the Tennessee side of both balds, and later assigned this grant to his sons, Zeke and Sam Burchfield.

Another Burchfield, Samuel (Smoke), married Mary Ann (Polly) Shuler, and brought his family to Cades Cove in 1866. His relation to the others is not clear. He could have been a brother to Wilson, who came to the cove about the same time. "Smoke" Sam Burchfield shot and killed "Chicken Eater" John Tipton in August of 1901. He was convicted of manslaughter and given a penitentiary sentence, but he became ill and was sent home, where he died in 1904.

Noah Burchfield and wife, Sara Brown Burchfield. Noah occupied the land bought by his father, Robert, in 1834.

A reliable account of the incident that has been handed down indicates that the shooting could have been more or less an accident. That "Smoke" Sam intended to kill someone was of little doubt, however. It was sort of a custom to have a party after a "run-off" of moonshine whiskey. Sometimes called

Nathan Burchfield, son of Sam Burchfield. Nathan claimed to have descended from a Cherokee Indian chief.

backins parties, these featured a quantity of the mash "back-ins," or spent beer, heated with spices, and served along with food. This particular backins party was being held at the Ike Tipton home, with "Smoke" Sam Burchfield among the invited guests. The alcoholic content of the drink is not high, but enough of it can elevate the drinkers' spirits. The Tiptons were Democrats, and "Smoke" Sam found himself among the Republican minority at this gathering. The Republicans had not fared well in the August election, and "Smoke" Sam was apparently taking quite a ribbing. He was not the type of man who could take teasing lightly. He left the party, to return an hour or so later with a pistol. "Chicken Eater" John Tipton agreed to go into the yard to see what was on "Smoke's" mind. As he appeared, "Smoke" shot him, as he probably would have done to any of the men to first meet him on his return to the party. He wanted revenge for his ribbing.

"Chicken Eater" John Tipton was married to the niece of "Smoke" Sam Burchfield and they had five small boys. Almost immediately after the killing, "Smoke" saw the significance of what he had done, and he tried several times to compensate the bereaved family with offers of financial assistance and gifts of land.

THE GREGORY FAMILY

The Cades Cove Gregorys descend from Russell Gregory (1795-1864) and Susan Hill of North Carolina. We do not know just when Russell Gregory moved his family into Cades Cove. His ownership of land is established by references in deed boundary calls and in estate settlements, but not from registration. He is listed in the 1850 and 1860 census, but not that of 1840, although he was a member of the Jury of View to mark out the road by way of Chestnut Flats to the Parson's Turnpike, and was appointed supervisor to construct this road in 1838.

The land transaction of record that does involve Russell Gregory is that of a partnership purchase in 1853, with Daniel D. Foute, John M. Coffin, and Richard J. Wilson, of an extensive area of land in North Carolina. This land, 1,550 acres, was along the state line and included a portion of what is now known as Gregory Bald. We know that Gregory built a house on the North Carolina side of Rich Gap and lived there a few years, but we do not know how many of his family were with him. In this partnership, Foute had one-third interest, Gregory one-third, and Coffin and Wilson shared one-third. After the Civil War, Wilson obtained the Foute and Coffin shares, but not that of Gregory. Russell Gregory was killed by a Confederate camp guard in December, 1864, possibly without his heirs knowing about the North Carolina land deal. The land was purchased from Wilson by Kitchens Lumber Company which logged the area early in this century. Upon transfer of titles to the State of North Carolina for the park, the Gregory family was contacted, but they decided that the cost of pressing claims would be excessive, so the title was declared clear by the courts.

Russell and Susan Hill Gregory had eight children. Of these, Druary (Drew) probably had the greatest influence on the cove population, raising ten children to maturity.

THE MYERS FAMILY

The Myers families of Cades Cove originated with John Myers (1792-1854) and Jane Dunn Myers (1792-1865) who moved, with the Dunns, into Tuckaleechee Cove from Horse Creek, Greene County, Tennessee, about 1821. John Myers became a fairly well-to-do farmer and was responsible for major developments of the Tuckaleechee Valley in the last century. Two of his sons, Daniel H. (1819-?) and John (Baldy) (1827-1906) began the Cades Cove elements of the family.

Daniel H. and Matilda Cable Myers lived and reared their family in Tuckaleechee Cove. After Matilda's death, Daniel married her cousin, Viney Cable, a daughter of Peter Cable. He died soon after this marriage and Viney cared for the younger children. His sons, Daniel H., Jr., Peter A., and Henry Abe married into Cades Cove families and reared their families there. (Dan Myers pictured with bee gums, p. 67).

A second son of John and Jane Dunn Myers was named John, and was differentiated by the simple way so often used in friendly groups of appending a descriptive word to the given name. Usually the appended word referred to an obvious

"Baldy" John Myers and wife, Mary Ann Tipton Myers.

characteristic. This John was known as "Baldy," and all references were as if this were a part of his given name, so Baldy John Myers he was. Women also were sometimes differentiated by an added name, since many women had the same given name or nickname, and some married men of the same surname. The usual way to distinguish these women was to add their husband's given name, such as: "Sis" Cassie, wife of Cassie Myers; "Sis" Jonathan, wife of Jonathan Myers; Mary Bob, wife of Bob Cable, etc.

Baldy John Myers married Mary Ann Tipton of Tuckaleechee Cove, and he moved his family to Cades Cove. Along with farming, he was a maker of fine furniture from black cherry and other hardwoods of the Smokies. He was active in the church and in local community and county politics. The population of Cades Cove during the first quarter of this century was dominated by the children and grandchildren of Baldy John and wife. Their first child died in infancy, but the remaining ten lived to marry and have large families.

THE SPARKS FAMILY

James Sparks from North Carolina bought land in Cades Cove from Thomas Tipton in 1835 and is listed in the 1840 census with a family of nine. He died late in 1840, but there is no marked grave for him in Cades Cove. His widow married Charles Fisher in 1845, and is recorded in 1850 as being in the household of Fisher with her six children.

Nathan H. Sparks was born in North Carolina. His relationship to James Sparks is not known. The present day Sparkses of Cades Cove descended from Nathan and Eliza Jane Potter Sparks.

THE POWELL FAMILY

There is very little information on the Cades Cove Powells. This family and the Chestnut Flats Burchfields were very closely related. They intermarried and lived in close proximity, rather isolated from the rest of the cove population.

William Riley Powell first appears in 1852, when G. W. Rowan recorded an unusual transfer of property rights to him. Powell was given full rights to the "plantation" for the lifetime of the elder Rowan and his son Charles, who was not able to care for himself, and at their death was to have title to the property. He was to provide for the Rowans and to maintain the "plantation" in a good productive state. Powell later purchased additional land from D. D. Foute and from Samuel Henry. These lands were located toward the eastern end of Cades Cove at Rowans Creek. Some of this property passed from his widow to the property of Dan Myers, which was sold for park purposes.

George W. Powell, son of William Riley, was a corporal (B Company, 6th Infantry, Union Army) in the Civil War. When he returned, he went to live among the Burchfields in the Chestnut Flats area and married Mary Ann Burchfield. He purchased land from Post heirs in 1878. He was a licensed whiskey distiller, specializing in apple and peach brandies. In the 1870s, he was in partnership with Jules Gregg, operating a corn whiskey distillery in the west end of the cove. After Tennessee outlawed the manufacture of whiskey in 1878, the activity had to cease from a legal sense, although as the newspaper account of September 18, 1878, suggests, Powell remained in this business for some time afterward. (See p. 55). George W. Powell, Sr., played some role in the affairs of the community, as his name is listed on juries of view for road allocation and as an official in local and national elections.

His nephew, George W. Powell, Jr., ("Little George") was married to Martha Gregg, a daughter of Jules Gregg. He was shot and killed from ambush on a Saturday evening in December, 1897, evidently because he had given testimony against parties accused of making moonshine whiskey. A newspaper account from the MARYVILLE TIMES of June 10, 1899, reports how another Sam Burchfield, not "Smoke," figured into this shooting.

MARYVILLE TIMES, June 10, 1899:
SAM BURCHFIELD ARRESTED
Charged with the murder of George Powell in December, 1897

Tuesday Sheriff Rule and Deputy Edmondson brought in Sam Burchfield from his home in the mountains. Burchfield is charged with the murder of George Powell in December 1897 for which Hale Hughes is now serving a 20-year sentence in the pen. The facts that led up to the arrest of Burchfield were as follows: A letter was received from Hale Hughes in which he stated that he and Sam Burchfield, who is his father-in-law, had made it up to kill Powell and each took different stands. Burchfield's was near the house. Hughes' stand was at another place. It so happened that Powell was at home and Burchfield, according to the story, did the shooting, although Hughes admits that if Powell had passed his way he would have killed him. It will be remembered by our readers that Powell was a witness against Hughes for running an illicit still. Sam Burchfield is a man of 60 years of age, according to his own story, although he does not look it. He is over 6 feet tall, has long coal black hair and a bushy head and moustache of the same color. He keeps his hair curled and takes as much pride in it as any woman. He has been, we are reliably informed, a well known moonshiner, and has been up before the Federal Court a number of times and rendered guilty.

Sheriff Rule and deputies are busy summoning witnesses, of whom there are 16, scattered all over mountains, some in North Carolina.

DR. JOHN CALVIN POST

Dr. John Calvin Post was apparently born into the New York Dutch family of James and Alyea Hawthorne Post, at Elmira, New York, in 1803. He was well educated as both a medical doctor and a mineralogist, but the latter seemed to be his first love.

In the early 1840s, John Calvin, along with two brothers, set out for the frontier. One brother, William, stopped off in Illinois. The other brother and John proceeded by river boat down the Ohio and Mississippi toward Tennessee. Somewhere on route, the boat's boilers exploded, killing several passengers, including the brother, and injuring Dr. John Calvin's leg to make a cripple of him for life. He somehow made his way to East Tennessee and to the home of William and Rebecca Wallace Thompson. William Thompson was a prominent Blount County resident. He had participated in a supervisory capacity in the removal of the Cherokees to the West in the 1830s. The Thompson home, a large two-story log house, later covered with weatherboarding, still stands as the "Brown House," a part of the Maryville College Campus. It was bought by a Reverend Brown who reared his family there. The farm was later acquired by the college, and the house is now being restored to become a historical museum.

Dr. Post remained with the Thompson family while he recovered from his injury. Romance bloomed with one of the daughters who cared for him, and Martha and he were married at the family home in 1846. Dr. Isaac Anderson, founder and president of Maryville College, officiated. The only son of Dr. Anderson, Samuel, was married to Mary Thompson, an older sister of Martha.

The object of Dr. Post's visit to the southern Appalachians seemed to be mineral exploration, and it appears from the records that he had made two previous visits to the area. He bought land and/or mineral rights over a wide geographical area, in northern Georgia, where he most probably visited earlier than the 1840s, in Roane County, Tennessee, and in western North Carolina.

The couple made their home for about a year at Eldorado, near a mining operation on the headwaters of Hesse Creek, on the road from Cades Cove to Tuckaleechee. He moved to

Dr. Calvin Post, medical doctor and mineralogist.

Cades Cove in 1847, and built a home for his new bride near the place where the Parson's Branch Road crosses Forge Creek in the western end of the cove. It seems that all their children were born at this place. Quoting from Miss Jessie Turner, a granddaughter:

Dr. Calvin Post created a homeplace in Cades Cove, which he called Laurel Springs. It was a kind of botanical garden; a horticultural Eden. There were beautiful native trees. There were walks and driveways bordered with trees. There were flowers in beds branching out from the house. There were acres in vegetable gardens, and other acres in fruit trees, apples, pears, raspberries, gooseberries, blackberries. There were crystal clear creeks which added charm and nature's own music.

Daniel David Foute, a major landowner in the cove.

Post taught his children astronomy and natural history. He was a very religious man and had a daily prayer hour schedule with which he would not let visitors or business interfere. A well educated man, Dr. Post associated, personally and by correspondence, with the intellectuals of his time. He remained a very personal friend of Dr. Isaac Anderson until Anderson's death in 1857.

Post was a Union sympathizer living in a "nest" of Rebel sympathizers in the western end of Cades Cove, and he was well known for his stand on slavery. Mostly due to harassment, he moved his family to Maryville, where he died in 1873.

Post had first bought land from James Quiett in 1846. In 1854, he bargained for the Calloway Grant lands of 5,000 acres and understood that the title was clear. However, after much litigation, Post's heirs discovered that the Calloway heirs maintained title to the lands, and the Post heirs did not.

The youngest son of Dr. Post, James W., acquired ownership of the homeplace and, through managing the lands of Morton Butler, maintained some contact with Cades Cove until the 1920s. J. W. Post operated saw mills in the cove for the first decade of this century. He was a builder and real estate developer, with extensive operations in Chattanooga, Tennessee.

DANIEL DAVID FOUTE

Daniel David Foute came to Blount County from Greene County to assist his uncle in the office of county court clerk. He later served two terms as circuit court clerk, during which time he became aware of lands available through tax sales and otherwise. He began to accumulate real estate in the vicinity of Maryville and throughout Blount County, especially in the mountains. His first major venture was the acquisition of the Montvale property (6,300 acres) and the establishment of a "Watering Place" at the mineral springs in 1832. From there he expanded south and eastward. To provide easier access from the south to the Montvale establishment, he built a road across the Chilhowees, through Happy Valley, to connect with the newly built Parson's Turnpike.

In the meantime, Foute was in partnership with Robert Shields and David Emmett (Emert) in building and operating a bloomery forge in the west end of Cades Cove. Emmett had built a grain mill, operated by Robert Shields, near the forge site. Shields also operated the forge. Shields had contracted with William Tipton and others in 1831 for the purchase of 1,600 acres in the southwestern end of Cades Cove, which included the mill and forge sites.

Foute was chartered by the State of Tennessee to construct a 4-foot wide horse trail from near his Montvale property (Six Mile) through the Chilhowees to Cades Cove, then following the old Indian trail up Ekaneetlee Branch to the state line at

Ekaneetlee Gap. Records show that the trail lacked about a mile of being completed in 1838. Later, the section from the Chilhowees to Cades Cove was opened for wagons and became the Cooper Road and a principal access to Maryville. Foute also opened, under charter, a horse path from Happy Valley to Cades Cove, again following an Indian Trail, and one from Cades Cove to the Parson's Turnpike, via the Chestnut Flats. Both of these were later opened to wagons by order of the county court.

Along with these activities, Foute continued to purchase land in Cades Cove as it became available, and to acquire untitled mountain lands through state grants. In the early 1850s he, along with Russell Gregory, John M. Coffin, and Richard J. Wilson, purchased 1,550 acres of mountain land in what is now Swain County, North Carolina. It included a portion of what is known as Gregory Bald. In 1856, Foute advertised 15,000 acres of land for sale in Cades Cove.

After retiring from his second term as circuit court clerk in 1848, Foute moved into Cades Cove to take over the active management of his properties. He first moved to a place on Rowans Creek. Later he moved to the western end of the cove

Dr. Thomas McGill, M.D., and family were in the cove between 1902 and 1905. There was a medical doctor in residence in the cove almost continuously from 1835 to 1914.

Many other people left their individual marks on the cove, though their names have since been forgotten. So it is, with the two unidentified ladies shown here in front of the Alec Wilson house.

to take over the Robert Shields property, mill, and forge. Shields could not meet his payments on the 1,600 acres purchased from the Tiptons, and Foute took title under bond to pay William Tipton and others the indebtedness. Until this time, a son of Robert Shields, Frederick, had been operating the grain mill. After Robert Shields' death, Frederick moved his family to the original Shields Sugar Cove, on upper Forge Creek. However, upon settlement of the Foute estate in 1866-1867, Frederick Shields purchased the mill site and several hundred adjoining acres at the court sale, and moved his fast-growing family "back home."

D. D. Foute was a Confederate sympathizer, as were all the members of his family, and after the "turn of the tide" in 1864, the family did not fare too well in East Tennessee. Foute was taken from his sick bed in Cades Cove to the Federal prison in Knoxville. His daughter pleaded for and got permission to take her father to her home, where he died a few days later, in January, 1865. He died intestate.

The Foute estate was turned over to the Blount County Chancery Court for settlement. The entire record of all his holdings, land and personal property, as well as indebtedness, is on file in the archives of the chancery court clerk. The principal purchasers of Foute's Cades Cove property were Frederick Shields, Henry H. Shields, Daniel B. Lawson, G. W. Feezell, J. W. H. Tipton, and Nathan Sparks. In fact, the entire Cades Cove holdings of 14,000 acres, except for fewer than 200 acres, were purchased by these individuals.

Remembering:
a trip back to grandpa's house
by Inez McCaulley Adams

*Who were these people of Cades Cove? Only a
few of them have been listed here. We know
they were an independent people – but not to
the exclusion of helping a neighbor; they were
God-fearing, for that was the religion of the
frontier; they were hardworking, laboring all
spring, summer, and fall to provide for their
families and livestock through the cold winters.
They were a hardy, intelligent people. A few
families accumulated wealth in land and
livestock. Many sent their children out of the
cove for education and to contribute leadership
in various professions. As in any community,
there were those who upheld and practiced the
higher norms of human interaction, and those
who preyed upon the good nature of others. But
mostly they were "just plain folk."*

*The people of Cades Cove are gone now and
their homesteads are disappearing from view.
Only a few people remain who remember the
cove as it once was. Some of us are trying to
record our remembrances before they, too, are
gone. Inez McCaulley Adams, daughter of the
Reverend Millard and Dulcie Abbott McCaulley
and a granddaughter of John and Rutha Myers
McCaulley, still remembers. She was born in
Cades Cove and spent her early childhood
there. For several years, Inez has been
collecting information about her family, taping
conversations with former Cades Cove people,
and recording her own memories and
sentiments as she visits the homesites of her
ancestors. The following is transcribed from
one of her tapes. The parentheses are my own
additions.*

November 9, 1969

The sun was warm for late autumn, but a chill was in the shadows. Frost had been on the hills several times already. A fading old road led off through the crisp leaves that were falling. It was a narrow old road with steep mossy banks and bushes of Rhododendron growing over it until it was almost dark in places. It crossed a little stream, crystal clear and edged with ferns. On it went, up the edge of what was once a field. For a moment I had the happy feeling of anticipation I remembered as a child — I was going to Grandpa's and Grandma's house!

Grandpa (John McCaulley) had bought this place in October, 1908, from J. M. Ledbetter. He bought seventy-five acres for $75.00. It joined the Gregg land and Post property, and along the top of Fed Ridge to the Shields place. Fed Ridge was named for Frederick Shields. It was quite a distance from Grandpa's in any direction to any of his neighbors. When he bought this land my dad (Millard McCaulley) was only three years old. They first moved into an old log house that was on the property. They lived there ten or twelve years, or until they built the house I remembered them living in. My dad and his oldest sister, Maymie, dragged logs off the mountain with a mule and helped Grandpa build the new house. It was not a log house. They had the logs sawed into boards.

A wind storm had blown down lots of trees over a large area, near the Henry Whitehead place, and Witt Roberts had moved his saw mill there. Grandpa and Daddy hauled their logs to that mill. Bob Cable built and operated a dry kiln at the site, and Mann Ledbetter moved in a planing mill. They finished enough lumber for several houses and barns from the blown down trees, and from logs hauled to the mill from other areas.

Grandpa's house was weatherboarded with unfinished boards, but the floors and ceilings were of planed lumber. However, the floor of the kitchen was of unplaned boards. Daddy helped Grandpa with the chimney, too. They hauled rocks in from a nearby field for it. They went to the Tipton's Sugar Cove one winter and cut a big mountain oak (Northern red oak) and blocked it into pieces to make boards for the roof. In the spring they hauled the blocks home with a wagon, making two trips a day until the job was completed. Daddy remembers killing seven rattlesnakes while they were hauling the blocks home. The roof boards (shingles, or shakes) were made with a froe and mallet and stacked in weighted piles to dry out. One section of the high porch which ran almost around the house was never floored because they ran out of lumber.

Six of Grandpa's children were born at this place. Eighteen years after they moved here, I, their first grandchild, was born. I walked along this November day thinking of many things far back in the past. Suddenly the road seemed to be swallowed up by the forest. I took a while to make out the dim outline of the road continuing as I had remembered it. But here were big trees in the middle of the road! How many years had it been? A dim outline of a trail turned off up a familiar hill. There was the rock wall that went all the way up the trail. But the hill wasn't steep anymore. It had been such a climb to where the front porch was. It all seemed so strange and different to me now. I soon realized that it was the steps of a little child that took me up that hill long ago.

I walked on up to where the house once stood and there were more big trees. Above the house was once a grass covered hill, where clumps of laurel and honeysuckle (azalea) bloomed and blueberries grew. Now it was covered with tall dark pines, reaching high up into the bright blue afternoon sky. I stood there, amazed at the unbelievable quietness around me. Thirty-three years had passed, could it possibly be? Through all the "new" trees I was seeing a trail. It led to the "upper fields" and on through the mountains for about three miles to where we had once lived. That was the "short cut" we walked to Grandpa's. I remembered some things about that trail: steep places that made my legs hurt; a swampy place where little poles had been put across the black mud to walk on; a few old fields and apple trees; penny royal that grew along the way, which we crushed the leaves of and rubbed them on our arms and legs to keep away the chiggers. It seemed like such a long trail for me, but when we got to the corn fields we knew that we were almost there.

Oh yes, the scare crow! I hadn't thought of him for years. He was always there, dressed in a tattered old shirt, an old black hat and faded old overalls. How lonely he always seemed to look.

I could see the high porch around the house. The highest part was never finished and I was never allowed to play there, but that is where the cats always stayed. I had spent many nights here. I remembered Grandma's gnat smoke in the yard late in the evenings. She put live coals in a bucket and covered them with old rags. The smoke made it possible for us to play outside after the sun went down. There was a special breed of black gnats (midges) that threatened to eat us alive! I remembered Grandma's black hair, and how she pulled it back on her head and pinned it up with giant sized hair pins. I never saw it any other way. I could see her in the kitchen, and her big fat biscuits full of blackberry jam. She always seemed so happy. I thought the house had the biggest fireplace in the world. Grandpa would put logs on the fire that looked like half a tree to me. It must have taken many days of hard work to get in enough firewood for a long winter.

Just below the house was Grandpa's bees. He had a roof built over the bee stands. At one time he had 150 hives of bees. Some of these belonged to Bob Cable. Grandpa had taken care of them for two years for half the honey and half the swarms. When they moved them back to Bob Cable's place, they took four hives at a time, at night, on a sled pulled by a steer. When I was a child, I thought Grandpa had a special understanding with his bees and they would not sting him. I may have been right. I could see him coming into the house with a big pan full of fresh honey, and I'll never forget how it smelled.

I looked over to the place where the barn had been. It was all in tall trees now. The barn I remembered was one that Grandpa had built. There was a much older barn that stood across the branch. There was also a corn crib that stood by the side of the little branch. A two-story combination log smoke and spring house was built over the small stream behind the old log house.

When Grandpa first moved to this place he owned a yoke of cattle (oxen, steers) which he worked in the fields. In a year or so he bought his first horse, a three-year-old bay, from John Hitch, near Maryville. Later he sold his yoke of cattle to Abe Myers and bought a pair of mules. Daddy was a small boy then, and Grandpa gave him the horse, whose name was "John." One year, after the hay was in and the corn gathered, John began to get lame in one foot. His condition got worse and they decided he had what was known as "swinney," evidently a disease of the muscles or bones. The treatment was to

John McCaulley House, 1936

rub the leg and shoulder with turpentine and run a hot flat iron over the area. Poor old John continued to fail and took pneumonia and died.

Grandpa built the barn before starting on a new house. He cut and notched the logs himself. Neighbors helped in laying them. Two log pens were built and "shed" logs were placed on top of them. They put in the hay loft floor, then built up the top section and roofed it. Several of the neighbors came to help with the roofing. The wives came to help with the cooking or brought baskets of food, and the men stayed with the job until the roof was completed. Some of the people helping with the roof of Grandpa's barn were Wade and Cassie Myers — they were Grandma's brother and father; Johnny Tipton; Jule Gregg; George and Russell Myers — George was the brother of Cassie; Bob Cable and Jerd Wilcox. Matt Myers, Louisa Tipton, and Bess (Shields) Myers were some of the women that helped Grandma with the feeding of the men.

I could see the garden spot. It had a picket fence around it, and a gate. It was near the old log house. Daddy had slept in the back room of that old house, and the cracks between the logs were so open that he would find snow on his bed in the winter. Across the branch was a field that went all the way to the top of the ridge. There was a trail to the spring; the branch where Grandma did the washing — somehow the stillness was alive, so many things were coming back to me. I was hearing again the enchanting tinkles of different sounding cowbells in the early morning fog. They had a magic all their own. The night sounds, like the hoot of a big owl over the ridge that could chill the heart of the stoutest child; night birds that sang so beautiful in the darkness; katydids and frogs, and many other sounds that I never knew that I could remember; sounds of voices and laughter of all my aunts and uncles who made so many hours of my childhood happy. It was all here. I remembered sounds of the wind, that special "Smoky Mountain" wind that would begin with an uneasy roar on the mountains before it swept into the valley. I remember how it would carry a voice that was calling cows in at milking time, and the mournful sound of a dove.

I felt a deep sadness about this place that day, one that I could never put into words. A way of life has vanished from us that can never return.

I just had to see the big white rocks that were behind the barn. They were special rocks that we played on when Grandpa lived here. Now they were covered with moss and resurrection fern, still the most wonderful rocks in the world to me, but seemingly not as big as they were when I was a child. There were signs of wild hogs all around and many deer tracks.

The sun had gone down behind the ridge; darkness would soon creep in and blend into the stillness over the few old decaying logs of the old house that was a home many yesterdays ago. I thought about the grief and sadness that comes to every family, but there was an overpowering feeling of the happiness and togetherness that this family had shared. There would be winters of cold and wind and snow, and springtimes that no one would see. Summers would come again and drift into lazy autumns. The leaves would fall, and in a few years all traces of anyone ever living here would be gone. Except for the ones that can remember, it will be a wilderness again.

I knew that the old house was gone forever, along with a Grandpa and Grandma that cannot be with us anymore, but for a little while time really turned back for me. As I walked away, I looked back through tears; and I knew that for me no matter how big the trees grow, or how many years may pass, through this great gift we humans call memory, back in the hills there will always be an old road that goes to Grandpa's house.

John McCaulley Barn, already abandoned when this photo was made in 1936, was only a memory when granddaughter, Inez, returned years later.

Soakin' in the Mountains

I CAN still remember when I was a small lad growing up in the cove, how my grandmother would stare off into space for what seemed to be hours from her rocking chair on the porch. "What are you doing Grandma?" "Ah, just settin' here soakin' in the mountains." Even amidst the chores of subsistence living there was time to appreciate the aesthetics of the mountains surrounding Cades Cove. Today, thousands of visitors come to the cove each year to "soak in" the mountains that rise in hazy blue splendor above the grassy meadows.

For more than a century those same mountains protected the culture of this hidden valley from change. But change was inevitable. The mountains were not high enough barriers to keep out long distance communication, the automobile and highway travel, the effects of two world wars and of America's increasing industrialization, and the creation of a national park. The quiet cove settlement that had existed here for several generations finally yielded.

Some people clung to their homeplaces as long as possible, even as permittees when the cove was taken over by the National Park Service. Most chose not to stay, and as soon as a farmstead was vacated, the evidence of its occupation was removed. Many of the finest old buildings were destroyed. The land quickly reverted to forest and the valley began to return to "natural" conditions.

Then, in the 1940s, the National Park Service recognized that the human history of these mountains was as worthy of preservation as the natural history. It was determined that Cades Cove should be maintained as open fields, and that, insofar as possible, its farmsteads should be restored to depict life in the cove from 1825 to 1900. The Cable Mill complex should be developed to show a business and community center in a secluded mountain area. Through these efforts, a representation of Cades Cove life remains for us today.

It can only be a representation — a synopsis of the Cades Cove story. We can never really recreate life as it was for the owners and settlers of this valley. We can never really know the Tiptons and Olivers, the Myers and Foutes, and the many others who walked here. Their time has passed; they left these lands for us. But if we let ourselves "soak in" these mountains, if we let our imaginations carry us back to another century, we can begin to feel the presence of these people. They are still the hosts and hostesses for our visit to Cades Cove.

APPENDIX A

CADES COVE LAND GRANTS (in order of filing)

GRANTEE	NUMBER	DATE (1800)
William Tipton	6730 (640 A.)	3/23/21
William Tipton	6731 (640 A.)	3/23/21
Jabez Thurman		
William Tipton	11806	9/25/25
Abraham Tipton	231	/25
Richard S. Shields*	3802	6/16/28
Thomas Jones	1417 (40 A.)	9/25/30
William Tipton	2789 (500 A.)	12/15/34
Thomas & Wm. Tipton	2812 (1255 A.)	1/16/35
A. C. Renfro	2910	11/5/35
Peck & Estabrook	22173	11/26/38
Charles Murray	3278 (5,000 A.)	11/ /38
Charles Murray	1738	11/24/38
William Murray	22174 (5,000 A.)	11/22/38
Daniel D. Foute	22386	2/11/39
Noble J. Tunnel		11/26/40
Louis (Lewis) Jones**	23588	8/13/40
Daniel D. Foute	23891	7/8/41
Daniel D. Foute	23893	7/8/41
Daniel D. Foute	23890	7/8/41
Joseph Calloway heirs***	3571	9/24/41
Nathan Rose	25308	6/3/45
Daniel D. Foute	23839	8/30/51
Daniel D. Foute****	23840	8/30/51
George M. Shields	29751 (240 A.)	5/24/56
Lazarus Oliver	29767	
Alfred Potter	30875	11/26/67
G. W. Feezell	40006	4/2/70
G. W. Feezell	40031	8/10/70
D. B. Lawson	40716	6/1/80
Calvin A. Gregory	40967	3/7/83
John P. Cable	40938	5/28/83
Calvin Post	4783	/83
Wilson Burchfield*****	1779 B1.Co.Ent.	11/21/84
William Garland	41084	10/10/85

| J. L. Stephenson | 42282 | 10/4/90 |
| J. W. H. Tipton | 42283 | 10/4/90 |

     * Original entry to Joseph Flynn, assigned to Shields who sold to Joseph Lambert.
    ** Sold to D. D. Foute 12/23/46
   *** Hiwassee District No. 3965, 5/25/30
  **** Hiwassee District No. 4059, 3/25/31
 ***** Assigned by certificate to Zeke & Samuel Burchfield.

NOTE: Cades Cove was a part of the Hiwassee District which was surveyed and set off into townships and lots while still in the state of North Carolina. Early land descriptions in Cades Cove referred to the Hiwassee District boundary calls, and in several instances to lot numbers.

Appendix B

LAND SALES REPORT

Transfer of Cades Cove property from resident owners for the creation of the Great Smoky Mountains National Park.

REPORT NO.	NAME	ACRES	PAID
7	Robert Cable	50.0	$ 900.00
10	Sam P. Harmon	32.0	1,700.00
11	Jake Garland	108.2	2,249.00
20	J. M. Ledbetter	130.0	4,000.00
21	Wade Myers	55.8	3,000.00
29	Arless Oliver	81.0	1,000.00
34	George Potter	49.1	1,850.00
39	H. A. Sands	1009.0	5,900.00
43	George Shields	493.0	15,000.00
47	Paul Wilcox	9.1	1,000.00
50	Johnnie Cable	70.0	1,850.00
57	Shade Tipton	85.3	1,500.00
60	R. R. Burks	206.5	3,350.00
62	H. R. Gibson Tipton	32.0	500.00
85	W. Laz Anthony	146.1	1,200.00
86	George H. Myers, Jr.	81.0	6,000.00
88	George Tipton	99.0	1,349.00
89	David Sparks	84.5	5,000.00
115	H. T. Schuler	124.4	2,499.00
141	James Johnson	9.2	800.00
145	John Wilcox	5.0	185.00
148	John Abbott & heirs 4/5 ins.	30.7	750.00
153	John Geo. Gregory	28.1	800.00
209	Dan Myers	119.5	3,900.00
214	J. A. Dorsey	7.6	150.00
221	John C. Tipton	156.1	3,000.00
247	W. J. Gregory	50.0	1,800.00
283	Milton Lequire	61.8	9,000.00
285	J. E. Gregory	99.6	4,000.00
286	Sam Sparks & W. E. Abbott	401.5	11,550.00
302	John Chambers	25.5	1,400.00
310	S. H. Blair	173.0	4,850.00

311	Grayson Tipton	71.1	3,500.00
314	C. B. Buchanan	115.0	1,300.00
315	Martha E. Myers, et al.	1.1	1,500.00
364	W. A. Gregory	198.3	3,000.00
370	Andrew J. Shields	42.5	2,500.00
389	J. R. Oliver	116.6	3,000.00
322	W. M. Gregory	6.6	2,100.00
323	Caleb Wilcox	22.0	800.00
336	J. E. Gregory	66.5	1,525.00
353	M. J. Shields, et al.	46.5	3,000.00
354	Andrew W. Shields	325.6	13,000.00
408	J. M. Ledbetter	47.75	——*
409	Rebecca Cable	587.5	——*
410	A. K. Gregory	72.5	——*
411	John Shea & Harry M. Shea	48.82	——*
412	Luther H. Cooper (widow)	42.5	1,200.00
415	George Myers & Wm. & John Gregory	290.3	4,329.92
428	John T. Anthony	340.8	——*
442	George H. Myers, Sr.	40.5 & 22.0	5,312.50
457	Isaac & W. J. Tipton	101.9	1,700.00
467	J. E. Gregory	1.4	
468	J. E. Gregory	2.8	1,500.00
470	Fonze Cable & Asa Sparks	122.5	8,450.00
544	J. V. Cable	33.5	1,750.00
545	Rebecca Cable	53.0	5,000.00
546	John & Jane Coada	16.5	1,700.00
547	Jordan Wilcox	20.0	899.00
548	W. A. & Martha Hill	128.2	10,000.00
549	W. A. Gregroy	78.5	7,500.00
551	J. S. Brown	82.5	2,750.00
611	George H. Myers, Sr.	81.0	1,085.00
613	Milton Lequire	39.0	1,000.00
704	John F. Shea	647.7	2,789.00
705	Wade Tipton	63.5	900.00
730	George H. Myers & W. & J. Gregory	116.0	1,500.00
731	Sam Sparks	153.5	10,000.00
737	W. M. Gregory	32.5	2,600.00
738	John Gregory	52.0	5,000.00
739	E. F. Ames, Trustee	160.5	
		13.6	2,453.00
740	Carl Gregory	16.5	300.00
741	J. W. Post	18.5	250.00

791	J. C. Myers	100.3	
792		24.0	6,000.00
793	John T. Cooper	120.0	5,000.00
794	Luther Lequire	59.2	7,250.00
795	Wm. H. Oliver	333.7	10,000.00
803	Sam Sparks	4.0	——*
804	John McCauley	72.4	3,000.00
805	T. H. Shields	87.5	8,000.00
816	D. H. Myers	32.7	2,000.00
819		13.2	
820	J. P. Myers	21.0	5,500.00
821		26.7	
832	J. M. Lequire	95.0	5,000.00
833	Charles & Goldman Myers	177.0	16,500.00
834	Maggie Myers & Geo. Caughron	75.3	
835	George Caughron	193.0	12,500.00
836	Noah Burchfield	162.8	9,000.00
839		5.2	
840	W. H. Myers	37.5	6,262.63
841		115.8	
838	Elmer Abbott	64.4	5,250.00
842	D. J. Lawson heirs	40.0	400.00
843	J. H. & Kara Gourley	158.9	5,500.00
844	G. W. Gregory	74.6	3,000.00
865	W. A. (Abbie) Gregory	3.5	450..00

Additional Land Purchases not included in the Report:

Rhoda Abbott	575.00 (487.0)	$ 22,700.00
Jane Burchfield	184.30	7,300.00
Leannah Chambers	188.50	7,000.00
Cowan Russell	211.60	7,100.00
Morton Butler Lumber Co.	25,243.75	483,500.00
Martha & Casper Cable	97.25	——*
Florence (Wilson) & John Cable	67.70	——*
A. K. Gregory	72.50	——*
J. W. Post	18.50	——*
George D. Roberts	31.00	230.00
Rebecca Cable	53.00	5,000.00
John W. Oliver	237.50	10,650.00

* Items paid for by the Smoky Mountain Conservation Association with private gift funds. The price paid is not listed in the report to the state.

APPENDIX C

The following excerpts from Russell Burchfield's record book of 1911-1913 show something of the variety of goods and methods of payment by a few individuals that are typical of a general store in the Cades Cove area. The spelling has not been changed from the record.

R. D. BURCHFIELD STORE RECORDS 1911-1912

RUSSIE WHITEHEAD			AMOUNT	CREDIT
Aug	2	Carried from p. 28	$17.55	
	2	Tobacco	.22	
	5	Credit by check		$ 7.70
	7	Tobacco	.25	
	11	Tobacco	.25	
	17	Tobacco	.25	
	19	Shirts, socks	.90	
	22	Tobacco	.25	
	25	Tobacco	.05	
	30	Shirt, Shoe strings	.53	
	31	Tobacco	.25	
Sept	7	Tobacco	.25	
	11	Tobacco	.25	
	14	Credit by check		10.00
	15	Soc & Suporters, Cartredges	1.15	
	25	Tobacco	.25	
	28	Tobacco	.25	
	28	Cough Syrup, Tobacco, Paper	.55	
Oct	6	Tobacco	.25	
	14	Settled in full		5.75
	26	Tobacco, Overalls, Sox, Shoes	4.45	
	28	Shoe strings	.03	
	28	Tobacco, Hankerchief, Turkeys	3.35	
Nov	4	Tobacco	.25	
Mar	1	Cartredges, Tobacco	.85	
	7	Shoes, Socks	3.10	
	9	Tobacco	.05	
	13	Tobacco	.25	
	15	Suspenders	.25	

			AMOUNT	CREDIT
	18	Tobacco	.25	
	24	Tobacco	.45	
	27	Candy, under ware, Tobacco	1.55	
	30	Box paper, Tobacco	.20	
Apr	6	Socks, tobacco	.75	
	11	Cartredges	.65	
	16	Tobacco	.25	
	19	Socks, Tobacco	.55	

HARVEY PANE (PAYNE)			AMOUNT	CREDIT
Jan	10	Coffee, Leather	.40	
	15	Credit by eggs		.25
Feb	9	Settled in full		.15
Jun	15	Coffee	.20	
July	7	Credit by chickens		.10
	19	Credit by wax (Bee's wax)		.05
	25	Bal on flour	.36	
	28	Settled in full		.41
Aug	11	Bal on Shoes	2.75	
	19	Credit by Abe Myers		2.00
	29	Credit by sang		.45
Sep	?	Meat	.25	
	13	Settled in full		.55
	21	Coffee, Lye	.25	
	23	Bal on J P oil	.10	
Oct	24	Balance on coffee	.09	
	17	Settled in full		.44
	24	Pance, Bal on meat	2.10	
	24	Credit by peas		.96
	28	Credit by peas		.56
	28	Bal on cloth	.06	
Nov	6	Settled in full		.64
	20	Coal oil, Hankerchief	.15	
	23	Credit by cash		.15
Dec	4	Settled in full		.15
	9	Cloth, Coffee	1.32	
	12	Credit by fur		1.08
	15	Settled in full		.24
	15	Bal on coal oil	.09	
	30	Settled in full		.09
	30	Bal on cloth	.60	
Jan	6	Coffee, Soda	.30	
Feb	1	Bal on Meat	.15	
	5	Credit by eggs		.17

			AMOUNT	CREDIT
	26	Credit by eggs		.32
	28	Credit by eggs		.21
Mar	7	Credit by fur		.30
	?	Credit by fur		.75

NOAH ABBOTT			AMOUNT	CREDIT
Nov	14	Meat, Coffee	1.50	
Dec	26	Cloth, Thread	1.05	
Jan	10	Settled in full		2.55
	20	Bal on cloth	1.48	
	23	Cloth	.93	
	23	Credit by cash		2.00
	30	Soda, Candy	.15	
Feb	7	Settled in full		.56
Mar	5	Flour	1.50	
	18	Nails, Soda, Turpentine, Gum, Castor oil	.85	
	21	Credit by cash		2.50
	24	Settled in full		.25
Apr	5	Lard Bucket, Shirts	2.20	
	12	Settled in full		2.20
	28	Tablet, Hat, Candy, Coal oil	.55	
May	2	Sugar, Mule Tobacco	.75	
	15	Bal on Cloth	.10	
	24	Bal on meat	.07	
	28	Settled in full		1.51
June	17	Honey cans	.80	
	20	Credit by cash		.70
	20	Fly paper	.10	
	28	Meat, Shirt	1.30	
July	7	Bell	.20	
	7	Credit by shirt		.75
	14	Gum	.05	
	17	Candy	.10	
	21	Tablet, Pencils, Chewing gum	.21	
	26	Leather, tobacco	.50	
	28	Meat, Candy	3.25	
	29	Shoes, Cloth, Hose	4.25	
	31	Credit by Chickens		5.80
Aug	1	Cartredges, Snuff		
	8	Settled in full		4.96
	12	Tobacco	.10	
	14	Slate	.10	
	25	Tobacco	.10	

JANE MODY (MOODY)			AMOUNT	CREDIT
Nov	8	Carried from p 106	19.31	
	8	Credit by cash		9.25
	9	Credit by cash		5.00
	13	Coffee, snuff	.32	
	14	Credit by corn		.32
	16	Snuff	.14	
	22	Lard, Rice, Sugar	.89	
	23	Credit by corn		.39
Jan	3	Quinine	.10	
	21	Coffee	.22	
	25	Credit by corn		.22
Feb	1	Bal on Lard	.24	
	4	Salt	.15	
	6	Credit by corn		.34
	8	Bal on buter	.08	
	15	Bal on coffee	.19	
	18	Corset	.50	
	24	Bal on cloth	.10	
Mar	1	Shoe Strings	.05	
	25	Nails	.08	
	25	Credit by corn		.06
Apr	14	Cloth	.72	
	16	Credit by Chickens		.72
	16	Cloth	.94	
	21	Credit by Corn		.65
	21	Snuff, Salt, Horseshoe nails	.15	
	21	Axel Grese	.05	
	21	Credit by Corn		.74
	21	Bal on Shoes, Stockings	.48	
	22	Hat	1.50	
Jun	12	Comb, coffee, laudnum	.40	
	14	Credit by Chickens		.40
	15	Credit by cash		1.50
	20	Enbordry thread, snuff, salt	.50	
	24	Nails	.19	
Aug	15	Shoes, Stockings (Elsie)	1.65	
	25	Washboard	.30	
Sep	4	Credit by Elsie		1.65

BIBLIOGRAPHY

Burns, Inez E. *History of Blount County*. Maryville, Tenn.: Published by the author, 1957.

—————————. *History of Coves in Blount County*. Publication No. 24. Knoxville: East Tennessee Historical Society, 1952.

Carpenter, Frank O. "A Hike to Thunderhead." *Appalachia* Volume VI, Number 2 (December 1890).

Edwards, Lawrence. "History of Tennessee Baptists: Primitive Baptists of East Tennessee." Master's thesis, University of Tennessee, 1941.

Edwards, Olga Jones, and Frizzell, Izora Waters. *The "Connections" in East Tennessee*. Tennessee: Washington College Press, 1969.

Fink, Paul M. *Early Explorers in the Great Smokies*. Publication No. 5. Knoxville: East Tennessee Historical Society, 1933.

—————————. *Smoky Mountain History as Told in Place Names*. Publication No. 6. Knoxville: East Tennessee Historical Society, 1934.

Gamble, Margaret E. "The Heritage of Folk Music of Cades Cove, Tennessee." Master's thesis, University of Southern California, 1947.

Jones, Jean M. "The Regional English of the Former Inhabitants of Cades Cove in the Great Smokies." Ph.D. thesis, University of Tennessee, 1973.

Ledford, James A. "Methodism in Tennessee, 1783-1866." Master's thesis, University of Tennessee, 1941.

Newman, Robert B. "Notes on the Geology of Cades Cove, Great Smoky Mountains National Park." *Journal of the Tennessee Academy of Science* Volume 22, Number 3 (July 1947).

Shelton, W. H. *A Hard Road to Travel out of Dixie: Famous Prison Escapes of the Civil War*. New York: Century Company, 1893.

Weeks, Stephen B. "Tennessee: A Discussion on the Sources of Its Population and the Lines of Immigration." *Tennessee Historical Society Quarterly* Volume II, Number 4 (December 1916).

Wilson, Charles W., Jr. "The Great Smoky Thrust Fault in the Vicinity of Tuckaleechee, Wear and Cades Cove, Blount and

Sevier Counties, Tennessee." *Journal of the Tennessee Academy of Science* Volume 9, Number 11 (1935).

Special Sources:

Church Records of the Methodist Little River Circuit. *Recording Stewards Book, 1849-1858*. McClurg Collection, Lawson McGhee Library, Knoxville, Tennessee.

H. R. Duncan Papers. McClurg Collection, Lawson McGhee Library, Knoxville.

Historical Records Survey: Inventory of Church Archives, Tennessee Baptist Convention. Lawson McGhee Library, Knoxville.

Parham Papers. McClurg Collection, Lawson McGhee Library, Knoxville.

Record of Appointments of Postmaster, 1832-1858, XIIa and XIV. Tennessee. National Archives and Records Service.

PHOTO CREDITS

The photographs used in illustrating *The Cades Cove Story* are drawn from the files of the National Park Service or generously contributed from family collections, many made by unknown photographers. We wish to thank all who supplied photographs for this purpose, and especially the individuals listed below:

Dean Stone, *p. iv*
Jim Ayers, *p. 23, p. 50, p. 93*
Adele McKenzie, *p. 52*
Johnnie and Kathleen Post, *p. 87*
Inez Burns, *p. 88*

Cover photo by Ken L. Jenkins